- Where should we hold our reception?
- Should we use a band or a DJ?
- How do we word the invitations?
- How will we ever be ready in time?

You're finally getting married! But now you've got other decisions to make—all in time for the big day! Planning a wedding is work, but it should be fun—and this is the book that helps you keep a cool head while you count off the details... and count off the days until a wonderful, one-of-a-kind wedding!

THE WEDDING PLANNER

The Wedding Planner

Produced by
The Philip Lief Group, Inc.

Diana Ajjan

BERKLEY BOOKS, NEW YORK

THE WEDDING PLANNER

A Berkley Book / published by arrangement with
The Philip Lief Group, Inc.

PRINTING HISTORY
Berkley edition / February 1994

ISBN: 0-425-14104-7

BERKLEY®
Berkley Books are published by The Berkley Publishing Group,
200 Madison Avenue, New York, New York 10016.
BERKLEY and the "B" design
are trademarks belonging to Berkley Publishing Corporation.

PRINTED IN THE UNITED STATES OF AMERICA

10 9 8 7 6 5 4 3

Contents

Introduction

Nothing in the world is single;
All things by a law divine
In one spirit mix and mingle,
Why not I with thine?
——PERCY BYSSHE SHELLEY

SHELLEY SEEMED TO INTUIT A SIMPLE YET IN-
spiring truth in his poem ''Love's Philosophy'': that all
things in the natural world mix, mingle, and unite.
Whether it's the sky meeting the horizon, or the brilliant
sunlight warming the earth, it is the ''marriage'' of two
elemental forces that nurtures, sustains, creates, and rec-
reates the universe.

And so it is with the marriage of two unique individuals, whose love is so great that they choose to become
''one'' with each other. Of course, this does not mean
that they surrender or lose themselves, but that they unite
to create a stronger, life-giving force.

The word ''marriage'' conjures a variety of thoughts
and feelings in different people. It is not only a union
of two individuals, but an extraordinary eternal commitment to building a life together. Marriage means *always* supporting, communicating, sharing, and working
together to overcome life's difficulties and to make the
relationship grow and flourish. There's nothing like a
wedding—so charged with emotions, transitions, and
change—to test and practice your ability to work
together as a couple.

Although weddings can be very public events, they
should, in some way, be as unique as the couple about

1

to be married. Maybe you've discussed wedding plans already, or perhaps your engagement was spontaneous or a complete surprise. In any case, you're bound to be overwhelmed with thoughts about your special day. Everyone knows the most common response to the news of an engagement: "Have you set a date?"

When? How? What kind? What cost? I hope this book will help you answer the many questions you have about planning your wedding, and doing it efficiently. I use the word "you" throughout the book to signify both partners, not just the bride-to-be. Both of *you* should work together to plan *your* wedding. Not only will it make the process easier, but it's a good way to begin a lifetime of joint projects and mutual effort.

The first step you should take after getting engaged is to tell all of the parents involved. Try to anticipate your parents' reactions, and be prepared to respond to them with clear and simple explanations that will help put them at ease. The most important advice one can give— which sounds cliched but is tough to follow—is to communicate openly and honestly. Open lines of communication are essential not only between the couple and the parents, but between both partners, and ideally, between both sets of parents. If you can talk through everything—questions, concerns, plans—the path to a wonderful wedding will be smooth and enjoyable.

Once you've apprised your parents of your good news, you'll want to share it with other relatives and friends. You might want to call some people, and tell others as you see them; or maybe you would like to host a party at which you can make a big announcement. Many people like to celebrate their engagement with a party of some kind. It could be a dinner with your parents and siblings; or you might decide to have a big bash for your families and friends. However you decide to celebrate, keep in mind that this is *your* special occasion;

this party, as well as your wedding, should reflect your own tastes and personalities. Let the festivities be a personal statement of your unique relationship and love for each other.

The single most important element in any good marriage is probably the ability to compromise. Both partners have to be able to give and take, to find a comfortable middle ground in the muddle of disagreement so that neither person feels as though he or she has "lost." Compromise will also be an invaluable skill in planning your wedding. Inevitably, you and your parents—or you and your partner—will disagree on something.

In order to avoid unneccesary conflict, it would be wise for you to decide as soon as possible when you want to get married and generally what kind of wedding you'd like to have. When you talk to your parents about your wishes and plans, try to be open to their comments and suggestions. Although it may seem as though they're being controlling or intrusive, try not to get defensive. Remember, as parents they have had an emotional investment in all of the major events in your life, and an "adult" event like marriage is no exception. Try to be sensitive as well to what your marriage means to your parents. On some level, they may feel a sense of loss as you "leave" them to embark on a new life with your own family. The process of planning a wedding will invoke a lot of different emotions in the people involved, and it will be up to you to handle everyone's feelings with sensitivity and understanding. In doing this you will be better able to control your plans in order to achieve the wedding you want.

Although you may need to employ the art of compromise as your plans progress, don't lose sight of your unique wedding vision. There may be some things you'll feel comfortable compromising on, while other issues will require you to stand firm and make clear your needs and wishes.

3

Introduction

A wedding is a joyous event, but it's no secret that the preparations can cause a lot of tension and stress. Some people get so wrapped up in the plans that they seem to forget what's really important: the very act of marriage. You should mark this event with the kind of festivities that *you* want—not what your parents want or what you think you *should* do. Your wedding should be a celebration that you will remember fondly for years and years to come.

No matter what kind of wedding you decide to have, it will require planning. This handy book discusses the major elements of a wedding and provides checklists and charts that you can mark and fill in to help keep your plans organized. The book begins with a checklist and timetable that will give you an idea of how far in advance certain preparations need to be made. Although this isn't meant to be a rigid schedule, there are some things for which you must allow a certain amount of time. For example, it can take as long as three or four months for an ordered bridal gown to be delivered; then you must allow ample time for fittings (possibly two or more). So if you intend to wear a bridal gown, you should start shopping approximately six months in advance. Again, the checklist is merely a guide, and you'll need to tailor it to your individual plans and needs. It is based on a traditional wedding with approximately one year of planning time. Of course, it you're planning a wedding in three months, each relevant task will need to be accomplished at a much quicker pace.

Whether your wedding is to be an intimate dinner party, a sunset cruise, a mountaintop marriage, or an elaborate showcase, you'll never plan another event quite like it. So . . . relax, take one step at a time, don't be afraid to ask for help, and most of all . . . ENJOY IT!

Timetable Checklist

THIS CHECKLIST IS A GENERAL GUIDE TO HELP you plan your wedding efficiently. It is based on a traditional wedding allowing approximately one year of planning time. Some of the items listed may not be relevant to your particular plans, and if you intend to marry in less than one year, you'll need to pick up the pace.

I. Things to Do Right Away

- Choose a date and time
- Decide on approximate size and style of wedding
- Discuss budget and division of expenses
- Talk to clergy and book ceremony site
- Book reception site
- Decide size of wedding party and ask attendants
- Request an engagement announcement in your local newspaper

II. Things to Do 6–9 Months in Advance

- Shop for and order bridal gown
- Shop for and order attendants' gowns
- Contact caterer and plan food/beverages

- Choose florist and discuss options for bouquet/center-piece/decor
- Audition musicians/bands and book them
- Hire photographer/videographer
- Begin forming the guest list

III. Things to Do 3–6 Months in Advance

- Shop for and order invitations
- Order reception favors if necessary
- Hire baker if necessary
- Choose men's formalwear
- Plan honeymoon

III. Things to Do 2 Months in Advance

- Confirm fittings for bride/attendants
- Order rental equipment if necessary (tents, tables, chairs)
- Mail invitations
- Arrange transportation for wedding
- Make accommodations for guests if necessary
- Organize legal documents: blood tests, marriage license, insurance, bank accounts, changing name if necessary.
- Purchase wedding rings
- Purchase attendants' gifts

IV. Things to Do 1 Month in Advance

- Confirm all wedding services
- Confirm honeymoon plans
- Plan rehearsal/dinner
- Plan reception seating arrangement
- Make hair/nail appointments
- Last-minute shopping

V. Things To Do 2 Weeks in Advance

- Arrange delivery or pickup of gowns
- Confirm number of guests with reception site/caterer/ baker
- Write place cards
- Request wedding announcement from local newspaper
- Organize everything you'll need on your wedding day: gown/accessories, bag of cosmetic necessities, marriage license, rings
- Confirm honeymoon reservations and pack

❧ 2 ❧

Taking the First Steps

Deciding When and Where

The very first step in planning your wedding should be to decide when you want to get married. You might be fond of a particular month or season, or your date might be a more arbitrary decision. There are some factors to take into consideration, however. For example, if you intend to have a religious ceremony, are there any holidays that might pose restrictions? If you're planning a large wedding with out-of-town guests, consider optimal travel times. Do you live in a region in which winter storms—or scorching heat—are a factor? As you try to decide on a date, keep in mind that certain months, such as June, August, September, October, and December, as well as holiday weekends, are very popular for weddings. Reception sites often book these desirable times far in advance, so it is best to be flexible about your date. Begin your wedding plans armed with several dates in mind, just in case you find that your synagogue can't accommodate your first choice, or that the reception site you've chosen is booked on Memorial Day weekend for the next two years!

The exact time of day you will get married is a matter of personal choice. Certain regions of the country have customary wedding times; for instance, evening weddings are common in the South. Traditionally, formal weddings are held in the evening, and semiformal or informal weddings can be held morning, early or late afternoon, or evening. Of course, the time of day may be determined by the type of wedding you choose. A seaside wedding would probably be much more enjoyable in the day than in the evening, whereas a candlelight ceremony would be most aesthetically beautiful at night.

Do you want to get married in a church or synagogue, or in a club or hotel? At your beach house, on a boat, or in an apple orchard? At your college chapel, or in your hometown? Deciding on the style and location of your wedding will be largely determined by the number of guests you'd like to invite, your religious beliefs, and, of course, budget restraints.

The Wedding Budget

If your parents will be footing the bill for most or all of your wedding, before you begin to discuss the budget with them, you should make clear to them your ideas regarding size, formality, style, and location. If you lay out your wishes right away, your parents will be able to think about what they can realistically afford, so that your discussions around budgeting will be productive.

The traditional division of expenses between the bride's family and the groom's family is laid out below. These guidelines, of course, were created for young couples whose parents are paying for the wedding. If you are older, financially independent, or have been living together for some time, it might be more appropriate for you to pay for your own wedding, in which case you can divide the responsibilities or pay for them all jointly.

9

Taking the First Steps

THE BRIDE/BRIDE'S FAMILY:

- Reception (including food, beverages, music, decorations, and professional services)
- Invitations/announcements
- Wedding dress/accessories
- Flowers for ceremony/reception
- Bouquets or corsages for attendants
- Photographer/videographer
- Rental fee for church if necessary
- Groom's ring
- Gift for groom
- Rental of equipment if necessary
- Transportation to/from ceremony/reception
- Gifts for bride's attendants
- Accommodations for out-of-town attendants

THE GROOM/GROOM'S FAMILY:

- Bride's engagement/wedding rings
- Marriage license
- Bride's flowers
- Groom's/attendants' boutonnieres
- Ceremony official's fee/donation
- Gifts for groom's attendants
- Gift for bride
- Accommodations for out-of-town attendants
- The honeymoon

In these difficult economic times, nearly everyone's pocket is feeling pinched. A wedding can be an enormous financial drain, especially if the parents or the couple have not saved for it in advance. Traditional formal weddings can cost between $10,000 and $15,000, while very formal affairs can cost $20,000 or more. Today, wedding expenses are often shared more equitably between the two families. The couple, as well, may be able to pay for some if not all of the wedding if they are financially independent and secure. If one or both of the partners are remarrying, it is appropriate for the couple to sponsor their wedding themselves. If a couple wants to contribute financially but cannot afford much, they might consider taking responsibility for the deposits required for all services.

The issues of money and budgeting can be very sensitive. Just think for a moment and I'm sure you can recall other occasions in which money became an obstacle or point of disagreement . . . paying for a car or college, perhaps? Be prepared to handle these issues tactfully. The best way to do this is for you to discuss the wedding budget openly with your parents. If your parents seem ambivalent about your plans, there may be a financial reason behind their reactions. Imagine how difficult it would be for a father to have to tell his daughter—who has her heart set on a grand wedding—that he just can't afford it. Think about ways in which you can help ease the financial burden—either by offering to pay for certain things yourself, or by being flexible about your plans and altering them to accommodate the budget.

The groom's family may offer to pay for expenses other than those that are their customary responsibility. In some cases, the bride's family may be adamant about assuming the entire financial burden. The groom's family should be told clearly and tactfully (ideally by the bride's parents) that the bride's family wants and insists on this arrangement. Depending on how close your families are, you might act as go-betweens in the budget discussions, or you might get together as a group to talk about the expenses openly. However you discuss the wedding budget, be sure that all parties understand and accept the arrangements that are agreed upon so as not to cause hard feelings in the future.

The Budget

Use the following chart to record projected costs (that is, what is affordable) for various services, as well as estimates. As each service is retained, record the actual cost and who will pay it.

	PROJECTED	ESTIMATE	ACTUAL	WHO PAYS
Reception (per person)				
Caterer Food Beverages Cake Servers				
Attire Bride Groom Rings				

	PROJECTED	ESTIMATE	ACTUAL	WHO PAYS
Florist Ceremony Reception Bouquets Corsages/ Boutonnieres				
Photographer				
Videographer				
Music Ceremony Reception				

The Wedding Planner

Rental Equipment
   Tents
   Tables
   Chairs
   Other

Fees
   Ceremony/Clergy
   Reception

Transportation

Gifts

Invitations

Honeymoon

Tipping Chart

When figuring out your budget, don't forget to take tips into consideration. The following chart is a guide for the amounts and the appropriate time to tip.

WHO	HOW MUCH	WHEN
Caterer, club or hotel manager	If not included in fee, 15–20%	Add to bill
Waiters, bartenders	15–20% of bill	Add to bill or pay maître d'
Coat check, lavatory attendants	50¢/guest or flat fee arranged in advance	Add flat fee to bill or pay maître d'
Florist, baker, musicians, drivers, photographer	15% for drivers; others 1–15% for special services only	Add to bills

| Civil ceremony officials | Usually a flat fee | Groom gives fee to best man, who pays after ceremony |
| Clergy | Usually a donation | After ceremony |

Engagement Announcements

Once you've shared the news of your engagement with parents, relatives, and friends, you might want to "go public" with it by placing an announcement in your local newspaper. You should call the newspaper to find out if they have any special requirements, whether they will accept a photograph (if you wish to include one), if they have a standard form for you to complete, and information about deadlines. If the newspaper does not have forms, type your own announcement, double-spaced, and submit it to the lifestyle editor.

A traditional announcement would read as follows:

> Joseph and Carol Baker of Tampa, Florida, announce the engagement of their daughter, Lynn, to Scott McGinnis, the son of Daniel and Jane McGinnis of Miami, Florida. A May wedding is planned. (*Or:* A spring wedding is planned. *Or:* No date has been set for the wedding.)

If your parents are divorced, one or both of them may announce the engagement, depending on the situation. You would need to adjust the wording accordingly.

Alternatively, you might want to announce your own

engagement, particularly if you are sponsoring your own wedding. The invitation could read:

> Lynn Baker, a clinical social worker, is to be married in May to Scott McGinnis, a psychologist at General Hospital in Tampa, Florida. Ms. Baker is the daughter of Joseph and Carol Baker of Tampa, Florida. Mr. McGinnis is the son of Daniel and Jane McGinnis of Miami, Florida.

❧ 3 ❧

The Ceremony

ALTHOUGH MOST OF THE WEDDING PLANS and hoopla usually revolve around the reception, it is the ceremony that is the essence of your wedding. The ceremony is the formal recognition—both spiritual and legal—of your marriage. Whether it is performed in a civil hall, a church or synagogue, or some other, less traditional place, your ceremony should reflect the significance of this event to you, as well as your own faiths and beliefs.

Choosing a Ceremony Official

If you know a clergy member whom you would like to officiate your wedding, you should contact him/her as soon as possible to inform him/her of your intentions and the date you have in mind. If you do not plan to marry in this clergy member's house of worship, verify that the location you have chosen does not pose any problems. If you do not know a clergy member personally, you can discuss your plans with the clergy at the house of worship you are considering; or if you plan to marry somewhere other than a traditional house of worship, contact a local church or synagogue (or speak to others who have been married recently) for a clergy referral. Finally, you may not choose a clergy member at all, but prefer to have a judge or justice of the peace officiate your marriage. It is equally important to confirm your plans with him/her early, as their schedules book up quickly too!

Where to Have It

Choosing the setting for your ceremony is an important and very personal decision. For some people, there would be no question that they would be married in their family church or synagogue. Others might choose to have their ceremony at the reception site. Perhaps your college had an intimate and beautiful chapel that you would like to use. Or maybe you would prefer to exchange vows in your family's home. Of course, there are those individuals who want to completely personalize their ceremony: perhaps a boat enthusiast who wants to marry on the high seas; or a scuba-diving fanatic who wants to "get hitched" at a fathom below. How would you like to exchange vows in a hot air balloon? If you're a true exhibitionist, you might get married during some nationally televised event—how about Times Square on New Year's Eve!

Of course, marrying in an unusual location does not make your ceremony any less religious, spiritual, serious, or real. As long as the person officiating is agreeable to the site, it is as valid as exchanging vows in a traditional house of worship.

No matter where your ceremony is performed, there are certain things you will want to find out about the location:

- Is there a changing room available?
- Is there a reception area accessible there too?
- If there is a reception area; are there requirements regarding food, beverages, or decorations?

- Is there adequate parking?
- Is there sufficient heat/air conditioning/protection from inclement weather?
- How much time is allotted for the ceremony? The reception?
- What is the seating capacity?
- Are there facilities for disabled people?
- Are there any restrictions regarding music, readings, dress, photography?

Creating Your Ceremony

Once you've decided upon a location and confirmed the availability of the clergy or official, you should think about how you would like to structure the ceremony. If you are having a non-religious service—it will consist of a welcome by the official, a brief talk about marriage, love, and family bonds, and the exchanging of vows and rings. If you do want your ceremony to include religious customs, additional elements and the structure of the ceremony will depend, of course, on your particular faith. For example, a Catholic ceremony could be part of a complete mass in which guests participate and take Communion. Usually the person officiating your wedding will have a general format and can suggest variations. Although your ceremony is being witnessed by family and friends, it is probably one of the most personal events in your life. Think carefully about how you can make this momentous event most meaningful to you.

Are there special songs, prayers, readings, or music you wish to use? Many couples like to include attendants or family members in the ceremony, either to sing or read. Readings do not have to be solely from the Bible, although your clergy can probably suggest appropriate scripture to use. You might have a favorite poem about love, relationships, or new beginnings that would be appropriate, or perhaps there is a passage from a novel you would like to have read. Peruse poetry books at your local library or bookstore. Poets from the Romantic Period (late 1700s to early 1800s) such as Percy Bysshe Shelley (see Introduction) are a good source of appropriate wedding readings. If you do have readings in your ceremony, it is nice to supply guests with a wedding program so that they can follow along. You might also consider adding other symbolic elements to the ceremony, such as lighting a unity candle (as discussed in Chapter 6), sharing a cup of wine, or asking your guests to join you in reciting a prayer or poem. Use your imagination, follow your heart, and your ceremony will depict your love and relationship to all of those present.

If you are planning an interfaith wedding, don't feel that you must be married in one faith or the other. Many priests, ministers, and rabbis will work together to perform an interfaith ceremony, including readings, prayers, rituals, and songs from both religions. An interfaith ceremony not only respects both sides of the family, but it demonstrates that the combination of your backgrounds will make for a culturally and spiritually rich relationship.

Your clergy member or official can probably give you a copy of traditional wedding vows. You should contemplate these words and decide whether they convey what you would like to say to each other. If these vows don't seem quite right, you might want to write your own. Spend some quiet time thinking about what your marriage means to you. What is it that you would like to promise each other? As you contemplate these things, jot down notes. Then review what you've written, and try to write up these promises in an eloquent way. You can say separate vows to each other, or your vows can be integrated. For example, you might be able to write them in such a way that one partner begins with a statement that is either expanded on or responded to by the other partner. If you do write your own vows, consider having them embroidered or written in calligraphy, and framed. At the very least, be sure to keep a copy of your vows, perhaps in your wedding album.

Be sure to discuss in detail the format of your ceremony with the person who will be officiating. Some churches and synagogues have specific requirements regarding music and decorations, and you'll want to iron out these details now, before you begin consulting with musicians and florists. Some religions also require couples to participate in premarital sessions or instruction. Although this may seem like an unwelcome burden in the midst of all your plans, think of it as valuable time you can invest in yourselves and each other. It is a chance for you to seriously contemplate the meaning of marriage—*your* marriage—and to raise issues and concerns that should be addressed before you make this major life change. Premarital sessions can help set the stage for a lifetime of open communication and trust. Any time and energy you invest in your relationship, in whatever form, is time and energy well spent.

How the Ceremony Will Proceed

How will your ceremony play out? Of course, it depends on how you decide to structure it, but traditionally speaking it will start off with about a half hour of introductory music. Just as the ceremony is about to begin, the music will stop and then the processional music will begin. (See Chapter 11 for music suggestions.) If you are getting married in a church or synagogue, the clergy will enter first, and then the bridal procession begins.

In a Christian or Reform Jewish ceremony, the groom enters first, either from a side entrance or walking down the aisle alone. If he prefers, he can be escorted down the aisle by his parents. The groom's honor attendant enters next, either from the side or walking down the aisle. Then the ushers enter, followed by the bride's attendants and her honor attendant. The flower and ring bearers enter immediately preceding the bride. The bride can walk on the arm of her father, or another close male in the absence of her father; or, she can be escorted by both of her parents.

In a Conservative or Orthodox Jewish ceremony, the procession is led by the ushers, followed by the groom's honor attendant. The groom enters escorted by his father on his left and his mother on his right. Then the bride's attendants proceed, followed by her honor attendant. The ring and flower bearers come next, and finally, the bride escorted by her parents.

At the altar or under the *huppah,* you can choose whether or not to have your parents stand with you. If they do not, the two honor attendants stand next to the bride and groom respectively. The ushers and attendants stand off to the sides. In a Christian or Reform Jewish ceremony, the bride stands on the left, and the groom on the right (this is if you are looking from the back toward the altar or *huppah*). In a Conservative or Orthodox Jewish ceremony, the positions are reversed.

The recessional proceeds in the reverse order of the processional, with the bride and groom leading the way. In a Christian or Reform Jewish ceremony, the bride's and groom's parents follow the wedding party out. In a Conservative or Orthodox Jewish ceremony, the bride's and groom's parents leave immediately behind the bride and groom.

Traditionally, the area to the left of the center aisle is the bride's side, and the area to the right is the groom's side: people sit on a side of the aisle corresponding to the position of either the bride or the groom. Today, this custom is not usually followed and people sit wherever they please. You should, however, reserve the first row of seats for your parents, siblings, and grandparents. The next several rows can be reserved for the other relatives, if you choose; or, you can simply allow free seating.

Once everyone has entered (assuming that this is a basic ceremony), the official will welcome the guests to your wedding. He/she will then talk about marriage, the joining of two families, or something similar. If the official has known you and/or your families for some time, he/she might mention this too. Once the official has spoken, other readings or songs are recited or sung. Then, the official will ask you either to say your vows (if you have written your own) or to repeat them after him/her. You will exchange rings, if you choose, as a symbol of your union. The official will then declare that you are married, and you may exchange a hug or kiss.

You may decide to run through the ceremony at a rehearsal a night or two before your wedding. Arrange this with your ceremony official and the site, and let all of the attendants and parents know in advance. Rehearsals are important for making sure everyone knows exactly what they are supposed to do. Afterward, a dinner or party—usually hosted by the groom's parents, though anyone can—is a nice way to thank your attendants and go out together one more time before the big day.

Your Ceremony

Officials:
  Phone: Fee:

Location:
  Time:
  Rental fee:

Music:
  Introduction:
  Processional:
  During:
  Recessional:

The Wedding Planner

Readings:

Wedding Programs:

Decorations:

Equipment:
   Aisle runner
   Huppah or canopy
   Altar
   Kneeler
   Other

Notes:

Conventional Order for Processional/Recessional Christian Ceremony

POSITION AT THE ALTAR

Honor attendant   Bride Groom   Honor attendant
Flower bearer   Ring bearer
Bride's attendants   Ushers

The Ceremony

PROCESSIONAL	RECESSIONAL
Groom's honor attendants	Groom's parents
Groom	Bride's parents
Ushers	Two attendants
Bride's attendants	Two attendants
Bride's honor attendant	Two honor attendants
Ring bearer	Flower/ring bearers
Flower bearer	Bride and Groom
Bride and escort	

Conventional Order of Processional/Recessional
Jewish Ceremony

POSITION AT THE ALTAR

Honor attendant	Groom Bride	Honor attendant
Ushers		Attendants
Groom's parents		Bride's parents

PROCESSIONAL	RECESSIONAL
Ushers	Two attendants
Groom's honor attendant	Two attendants
Groom and parents	Two honor attendants
Bride's attendants	Flower/Ring bearers
Bride's honor attendant	Groom's parents
Flower/Ring bearers	Bride's parents
Bride and parents	Bride and Groom

❧ 4 ❧

The Reception

YOU'VE PLANNED AN EXQUISITE CEREMONY—
the readings, prayers, songs, and vows to each other.
Now it's time to *celebrate*!

Sit back, close your eyes, and try to imagine the perfect reception—the kind of wedding you've always
dreamed of . . .

Would it be an intimate dinner at a renowned four-
star restaurant, or a cozy meal at a country inn?

Would you have your reception in a hotel or in a
traditional reception hall?

Perhaps you've planned a seaside ceremony, and
you'll invite guests back to your beach house for a good
old-fashioned barbecue.

Or maybe the country is more your style, and you've
set your entire wedding—ceremony and reception—in a
lush green apple orchard.

You might have your reception on a yacht, or right at
home, in your parent's backyard.

As long as the location is comfortable and enjoyable
for your guests, you may choose any site you wish—
whatever is most meaningful to you!

The Reception

Choosing a Special Place

As you search for the perfect location for your reception, consider the following questions:

- What is the rental fee and what does it include?
- Is there adequate space and seating capacity?
- Are there restrictions regarding children?
- Will other weddings be held simultaneously, and is there adequate privacy?
- What are the hours of the reception? What is the overtime charge, and when does it begin?
- Is there a bridal suite available?
- Is there an area in which guests can wait for the reception to begin?
- Is it possible to have the ceremony there too?
- What services does the location provide, and if you prefer, can you provide your own?
- How big is the dance floor? Is a band permitted? Are there any restrictions regarding music?
- Are the grounds suitable for picture taking?
- Is there adequate parking?
- Are there facilities for the disabled?
- Is there adequate heat/air conditioning/shelter from inclement weather?

What Kind of Reception?

The overall style of your wedding will help determine the format of the reception. If you're having a traditional affair, you'll probably have a cocktail hour and full dinner—either buffet or seated—as well as dancing, the cake-cutting ritual, and any other wedding traditions you wish to include. Of course there are several alternatives that may suit you—and your budget—quite well. For example, an early morning ceremony followed by a champagne brunch would be lovely. You might plan an afternoon wedding followed by a reception of cocktails, hors d'oeuvres, and cake. Or you might like to have a midday ceremony followed by an elegant afternoon tea.

The Receiving Line

Before you begin the festivities at your reception, it is customary for you to greet all of your guests in a receiving line. If your ceremony and reception are at two different locations, you should form your receiving line immediately after the ceremony, before you proceed to the reception. Traditionally, the receiving line includes the bride's mother, the groom's mother, the bride, the groom, the bride's honor attendant, and the bridesmaids (in that order). The fathers and groomsmen usually mingle with the guests. However, you should create your receiving line however you wish! Maybe you want to have all of the parents present in the line, and have all of your attendants mingle with the guests (unless any of them are siblings and wish to join the line). With this custom, as with other facets of your wedding, do what is most comfortable and acceptable to all.

You might want to prepare in advance for your receiving line, particularly if there will be a lot of people at your wedding whom you do not know very well. If this is the case, review the guest lists with your families to refresh your memories on names. If it is helpful, peruse photo albums to try to connect faces with names. On the receiving line, if you do forget someone's name, simply smile and thank them for coming, or apologize and ask their name. You should introduce yourselves to guests you do not know.

How the Reception Will Proceed

If you have not had photographs taken prior to the wedding, you'll probably begin having them taken during the cocktail hour. Many couples choose not to have photographs taken beforehand because they don't want to spoil the awe and surprise of seeing each other in their wedding finery. However, be prepared to spend a significant portion of your cocktail hour—and possibly even the first course of dinner—posing for photographs. Think about this carefully before saying no to early photo sessions, particularly if your reception is going to be shorter than the usual four or five hours. Your wedding day goes by extremely fast, so you'll want to have as much time as possible to enjoy your celebration.

After the cocktail hour, the doors to the dining area will be opened and guests will find their seats. Restaurants, hotels, and reception halls usually provide you with a maître d' to be host of your wedding. If there is no maître d', consider asking a relative of friend if they would be willing to supervise the affair, handle the caterer's questions, assist guests, and so on. Once your guests are seated, the maître d', host, or bandleader might introduce you and your wedding party. Then the host will announce your first dance as a married couple. Traditionally, the bride next dances with her father while the groom dances with his mother-in-law; then the bride dances with her father-in-law and the best man, while the groom dances with his mother.

If you do not want to follow these traditional dance steps, you can simply dance together as a couple, then the bride can dance with her father and the groom can dance with his mother. Once the family has danced in the limelight, the host or bandleader will ask guests to join you. You might consider inviting guests to join in some ethnic dances during the course of the reception, such as Polish polkas or Italian or Israeli folk dances. If things go well, you'll be cutting up the rug all day or evening long!

Depending on the nature of your reception and your religious beliefs, you might want to say a prayer or blessing before any food is served. Consider asking a relative to lead the blessing, or if your clergy is present, it would be appropriate for him or her to have the honor.

Most wedding receptions, no matter what size or kind, include toasts to the newly married couple. The groom's honor attendant usually proposes the first toast at some point during the reception, after champagne has been served. The bride's honor attendant might propose a toast, and the groom might toast his new wife or their parents; or perhaps the bride and groom each want to toast his/her own parents.

Some other reception rituals include the cake cutting and the tossing of the bridal bouquet and garter. Often the band will play special music for the cake cutting as the bride and groom take turns cutting the cake and feeding often huge bites to each other. Toward the end of the reception—when the partying and fun are in full swing—the bride throws her bouquet (or a separate one made especially for this) to single women guests. The groom then removes the bride's garter and throws it to eligible bachelors. The antics really begin as the two lucky catchers take center stage: the man slips the garter on the woman who caught the bouquet, as the band cheers them on with some rollicking music. Of course, if you feel that the garter and bouquet toss is an outdated or sexist custom, you should feel free to eliminate it from your reception.

The reception is a time of celebration and entertainment, and the festivities need not end at dining, dancing, and the usual rituals. Maybe you have a friend who plays guitar and another who sings; if they are willing, why not pair them up to perform a duet? Do you have among your guests a juggler who would like to put on a show? You might consider hiring a mime, a clown, or a comedian, but be sure to preview their acts! You can have wandering musicians to serenade your guests, and if your wedding has a particular theme, perhaps the servers would be willing to dress in appropriate costumes. For something more extravagant, consider hiring a skywriter to scrawl a message across the sky, or plan an evening fireworks show! You can be as creative as you want with your reception festivities, provided, of course, that they are in good taste and appealing to the crowd at large.

The Seating Arrangement

Planning the seating arrangement for a formal reception usually requires lots of patience and juggling of names. You should save this task until the last few weeks before the wedding so that your confirmed guest list is as complete as possible. This will avoid your having to shuffle and reshuffle the seats.

As the guests of honor, you can choose to sit at your own table, or you might sit at a table with your attendants and their dates. Usually the bride's and groom's parents each sit at tables with their respective parents and other immediate family members. As far as seating the rest of your guests, it's really just a matter of common sense and a little thought. For instance, if you have two cousins who you know do not get along, try not to seat them together. As you do your seating plan, think about who would get along with whom; or which friends from different periods of your life you might want to get acquainted. If there will be several children and/or young adults at the reception, you'll need to decide whether to seat them together or with their parents. It would probably be more fun for the teenagers to sit together, but a group of younger children sitting together could be hard to manage. You might want to consult with the children's parents or with the teenagers themselves to find out if they have a preference regarding where they will sit.

Depending on the size of your wedding, tables will usually accommodate eight to twelve people. Your maître d'or host can help you decide how many tables and what size you'll need, as well as give you a floor plan showing the layout of all tables and where the band (or DJ) will be situated.

There is usually a small table set up outside of the reception room for place cards. These show the guests' names and table numbers. You might also want to put a guest book out on this table for people to sign as they arrive. A nice alternative to the traditional guest book is a blank book guests are asked to sign, write, or draw in!

If you're not planning a traditional formal wedding, the seating arrangement can still be preplanned, or you might just allow guests to sit where they please. If you're having a small reception, you might use place cards at each seat and guests can find their own places. If it's an informal wedding, an afternoon tea, or cocktail-hour-only affair, the seating can just be a free-for-all.

Guest Accommodations

If you will have several out-of-town guests, be sure to reserve a block of rooms in a hotel convenient to the ceremony and reception. Hotels often give discounts on multiple-room reservations. Do this well in advance to make sure you've secured adequate accommodations. Once your guest list is confirmed, you might be able to relinquish some of the rooms if you find you don't need all of them. Be sure to include reservation information and prices with invitations sent to out-of-town guests. If you can, arrange transportation from the airport or train station to the hotel. Check with the hotel first to find out if they provide cab or van transportation for guests. Finally, it's always thoughtful to leave a small welcoming gift in each guest's room—either some home-baked cookies, a basket of fruit, something appropriate to the wedding festivities, or some other more personalized gift.

Reception Services

When you search for a reception site, consider whether you want a place that will provide food, beverages, and servers, or whether you will have to hire a caterer, waiters, and waitresses. Inquire whether the site can accommodate special dietary needs (no-salt, low-calorie, low-cholesterol, vegetarian, kosher food), and inspect facilities for disabled people. Some reception sites have house bands, photographers, and florists you can contract as a package deal. This may be convenient and suitable to your needs; but if you have the time and inclination, shop around for different services—not only for price comparison, but also for quality.

The separate wedding services—catering, music, photography, flowers—will be discussed in detail in subsequent chapters. Whenever you decide to retain a particular service, be sure to get a detailed contract from the vendor that includes the names of the service providers, the hours to be worked, overtime charges, explicit services to be provided, fees, gratuities, deposits, payment schedule, and the cancellation policy. Read all contracts carefully, and make sure that the vendor signs as well. It's smart business on your part to pay small deposits and to make sure that cancellation fees are reasonable.

Your Reception

OPTION #1

Location:
Address:
Phone:
Contact person:
Price per person:
Dates available:

The Wedding Planner

Services available/costs:
   Photographer:
   Band:
   Florist:

Food:
   Cocktail hour
   Buffet or sit-down dinner
   Wedding cake

Beverages:
   Open bar
   Wine/Champagne
   Soft drinks

Servers:
   Waiters
   Bartenders
   Valets

OPTION #2

   Location:
   Address:
   Phone:
   Contact person:
   Price per person:
   Dates available:

Services available/costs:
   Photographer:
   Band:
   Florist:

Food:
   Cocktail hour
   Buffet or sit-down dinner
   Wedding cake

The Reception

Beverages:
Open bar
Wine/champagne
Soft drinks

Servers:
Waiters
Bartenders
Valets

OPTION #3

Location:
Address:
Phone:
Contact person:
Price per person:
Dates available:

Services available/costs:
Photographer:
Band:
Florist:

Food:
Cocktail hour
Buffet or sit-down dinner
Wedding cake

Beverages:
Open bar
Wine/champagne
Soft drinks

Servers:
Waiters
Bartenders
Valets

The Wedding Planner

Rental Equipment

Store:
Address:
Phone:
Contact:

ITEM	NUMBER NEEDED	PRICE
Tables		
Chairs		
Tents/Canopy		
Lights		
Audio/Visual		
Linens		
China		
Flatware		
Glassware		
Dance floor		
Podium		
Kneeler		

Total Cost:
Order By:
Delivery or pickup?   Time:

Money-Saving Tips

- A weekday wedding will probably cost less than a weekend.
- Morning or afternoon receptions are usually less expensive.
- Instead of a full meal, serve hors d'oeuvres, cocktails, and cake.
- Church halls, temples, community centers, and private homes can be less costly than reception halls, hotels, clubs, or restaurants.

❦ 5 ❧

Wedding Customs
and Traditions

WEDDING CUSTOMS HAVE EXISTED SINCE THE
early ages to symbolize the joy and everlasting commitment of marriage. While many of these customs have
remained intact, their significance has evolved over time
to reflect society's changing values. Following are the
origins and meanings behind some universal as well as
ethnic wedding customs.

Contemporary Universal Customs

Wedding rings: Since the time of the early Egyptians,
the ring which was made of leather, metal, or carved
stone, has symbolized unending love. The tradition of
wearing the wedding band on the third finger of the left
hand evolved from the ancient belief that the vein in this
finger ran directly to the heart. While it is customary for
British and American couples to wear their rings on the
third left finger, many European couples wear their rings
on the third finger of the right hand.

White bridal gowns: In early Roman culture, white symbolized celebration; in the Victorian era it represented
affluence. It wasn't until the beginning of the twentieth

century, however, that white came to symbolize purity. For some contemporary women, wearing a white gown is an important part of a traditional wedding. Other women today who are planning less traditional weddings choose to wear colors other than white.

The bridal veil: Traditionally, the bridal veil symbolized virginity, and in some Arab and Asian countries today, the custom of the bride wearing a veil until after the marriage ceremony is still followed. Early Greek and Roman brides wore red veils, which they believed would fend off demons. Early Christian brides wore either white or blue veils, to symbolize purity and celebration. Although contemporary brides might wear veils as decorative elements of their headpieces or hats, many choose not to cover their faces with them.

Wedding bouquets and flowers: Flowers at weddings have represented different things throughout history (as discussed in Chapter Ten). They were often used to symbolize fidelity, or strong herbs would be used to ward off evil spirits. Today, while some couples might consider the "language of flowers" in their selections, flowers and plants generally reflect the joy and beauty of the celebration.

Bridal party attire: There actually was a reason, albeit superstitious, for the bridal party to dress in similar fashion—to prevent an evil onlooker from placing a curse on the bride and groom. If the members of the bridal party looked like the bride and groom, an evil wisher would not be able to tell who was who. While it is still common for the attendants to dress similarly to the bride and groom, it is acceptable to vary the colors and styles of the attendants' dresses, and to have the groom's attendants wear accessories in a color different from the groom's.

The Bridal Shower: Dutch folklore tells that a father objected to his daughter marrying a poor man, and therefore refused to give her a dowry. The bride's friends "showered" her with gifts so she could marry and set up her new home.

"Giving away" the bride: The significance of this custom has fortunately disappeared in contemporary society. Traditionally, when a woman had few personal rights, she was literally "given away" by her father to another man. While many brides may still have their fathers escort them down the aisle, the practice does not symbolize the traditional concept of "giving away." In order to abolish this custom for good, some couples choose to walk down the aisle with both of their parents; to walk individually and unescorted; or to walk together. During the ceremony, the official might ask, "Who gives this woman to be married to this man?" to which the bride's parents would respond, "We do." If you wish, you may ask the official to change the question to, "Who supports this man and this woman in this marriage?"

Breaking a glass in a Jewish ceremony: It is customary at the end of a Jewish marriage ceremony for the groom to stomp on a wineglass wrapped in a napkin or handkerchief. This is not done for good luck, as is commonly believed, but to represent the destruction of the Holy Temple in Jerusalem, as well as other hardships endured by the Jewish people. Some couples also include the breaking of a plate, the symbolic hope that the marriage will last for as long as it takes the pieces to come together.

The wedding cake: In early Roman times, wheat symbolized fertility, and so a thin cake was broken over the bride's head at the end of the ceremony. Although the symbolism of the wedding cake is not clear today, it's probably safe to say that the tradition has prevailed because everyone enjoys a sweet piece of cake after dinner!

The groom's cake: This is traditionally a dark fruit cake, though today it can be whatever type of cake you choose. The groom's cake can be served along with the wedding cake, or it can be cut up and boxed for guests to take home. Tradition says that an unmarried guest who puts a piece of groom's cake under his/her pillow will dream of a future spouse.

Throwing rice: In Asian cultures rice symbolizes a "full pantry," while in other cultures it represents fertility. Today, the tradition of throwing rice at the bride and groom symbolizes the hope of an abundant life. Many couples, however, insist that their guests throw birdseed or flower petals, since rice can be dangerous to birds who eat it.

The honeymoon: This word originated from a Teuton custom in which couples drank fermented honey for thirty days after their wedding, or until the moon waned. Honey is a traditional symbol of life, health, and fertility. Today, the honeymoon allows the couple time alone to relax and enjoy each other's company without the intrusions of everyday life.

Carrying the bride over the threshold: An age-old superstition held that demons waited at the threshold of a new home. The bride was lifted up over them to protect her from them. Today, a groom might carry his bride into their home for fun, though most couples probably no longer follow this custom.

Ethnic Wedding Customs

You may want to include some of your own cultural traditions in your wedding celebration, or you might borrow from another culture if a particular custom appeals to you.

Wedding Customs and Traditions

African: Many tribal couples marry by binding their wrists together with grass. You could modify this tradition by holding hands as you walk in the recessional. Consider having the wedding party, clergy, or guests wear traditional African robes. Another custom, which probably originated in the American South, is called "jumping the broom." The couple jumps over a flower-adorned broom to represent their jumping over the threshhold into married life.

American Indian: A Native American bride's dress can be woven in the colors representing the directions of east, south, west, and north: white, blue, yellow, and black respectively. Ceremonies usually take place facing the east, as this is the direction that indicates the future. Another custom is to mix together yellow and white corn meal, representing female and male respectively, and eat this during the ceremony to symbolize the union of marriage.

Amish: Amish weddings usually take place after the harvest, during the middle of the week. It is customary for the couple to deliver each invitation in person.

Austrian: Brides traditionally include myrtle, which symbolizes life, in their veils or headpieces.

Belgian: A bride embroiders her name on her handkerchief, which she keeps or frames and displays until the next woman in the family is married. This woman then adds her name to the handkerchief, and passes it to the next woman who is married.

Bermudan: Traditionally and even today, some couples adorn their wedding cake with a sapling, which they plant at the reception.

Chinese: Red and gold are popular colors for Chinese brides, as they represent happiness and wealth. Traditionally, two glasses of wine and honey are tied with a red ribbon, and the couple drinks from these cups. You can use red throughout your wedding, in centerpieces, bouquets, boutonnieres, and to wrap your attendants' gifts.

Croatian: After the ceremony, the bride's mother replaces the bride's headpiece with a kerchief which signifies that she is now married.

Czechoslovakian: Brides traditionally wore wreaths of rosemary, which symbolizes loyalty and love. After the ceremony, a ribbon is stretched across the sidewalk and guests must pay money to allow the newly married couple to pass by.

Dutch: Dutch couples used to be honored at a party prior to the wedding, at which they would sit under a canopy of evergreens symbolizing eternal love and receive their guests' good wishes. After the wedding, the couple would plant lily of the valley, and when it bloomed each year they would renew their vows of love.

English: The couple and their wedding party used to walk to the ceremony, following a young girl who would strew flower petals along the path. If it is feasible, consider walking to your ceremony, or from the ceremony to the reception. Traditionally, the bride's attendants were all young girls, and the groom did not have attendants. The bride used to carry a decorated horseshoe on her arm for good luck.

Finnish: Brides traditionally wore golden crowns. After the wedding, single women would dance around the blindfolded bride, who would place the crown on one of their heads. Like the traditional toss of the bridal bouquet, this crowning predicted who the next bride would be.

French: Many French couples drink their toast from a special two-handled cup which is passed on through generations. If you do not have one in your family, you might want to purchase a silver cup, have it engraved with your initials, and keep it for your children to use.

German: The couple holds candles adorned with flowers and ribbons, a tradition that can easily be incorporated into contemporary weddings. Consider the custom of riding to your wedding in a carriage drawn by black horses.

Greek: Traditionally, the groom's godfather participated in the ceremony; today, he is often the groom's honor attendant. He assists in crowning the couple, and in the ritual of circling the altar three times. At the reception, candy-coated almonds, which represent fertility, are bundled in tulle and given as favors.

Indian: At the end of the ceremony, the groom's brother would sprinkle flower petals on the couple to ward off evil spirits. Either before or after the ceremony, consider having a few relatives or friends hand a flower to each guest.

Irish: The customary Irish wedding cake is a rich fruitcake. Consider serving this instead of a traditional wedding cake. The claddagh, or wedding ring, is formed of two hands holding a heart with a crown above it. When the ring is worn so that the hands face in, it indicates that the bride is married.

Italian: It is an old Italian custom to toss "confetti"—sugared almonds—at the bride and groom. You might want to place a plateful of these almonds on each table, or include them in favors for your guests. The traditional Italian dance to do at your reception is the tarantella.

Japanese: Traditionally, Japanese couples take nine sips of sake at their reception to signify that they are now a married couple. At your reception you might want to include kyogashi, colorful candy in the shape of flowers or something else, as a sign of celebration. Since red is the color of joy and luck, you might want to incorporate it into your attire, flowers, and decorations.

Jewish: It is a Jewish custom to have a ketubbah, a marriage contract that is written and decorated by an artist. The ketubbah is displayed at the wedding and then hung in a prominent place in the new couple's home. You might want to get married under a *huppah*, the traditional Jewish wedding canopy.

Korean: Since the groom used to ride to the bride's house on a white horse, consider traveling to your wedding in a horse-drawn carriage. You might want to place on each table plates of dates and chestnuts, which symbolize fertility and happiness.

Lithuanian: The parents of a newly married couple traditionally served them a symbolic meal: wine for joy, salt for tears, and bread for work. You and your families might consider including these symbols at your reception, as well as preparing other ethnic foods.

Mexican: A fun and festive Mexican tradition that still takes place today is for guests to form a heart-shaped ring around the couple, who dance together in the middle. The Mexican ceremony also includes the blessing of an arras, a small chest filled with gold coins, which symbolizes strength and wealth. The groom also gives the bride thirteen coins as a symbol of his commitment to her.

Philippino: It is customary in Philippino weddings for a white silk cord to be draped around the couple's shoulders. You can symbolize your union in this traditional way, or by lighting a unity candle during your ceremony. Traditionally, the groom's family paid all of the wedding expenses and the bride's family gave the couple a cash dowry.

Wedding Customs and Traditions

Polish: Polish brides traditionally wore decorative aprons with pockets over their gowns in which guests could tuck monetary gifts.

Puerto Rican: A custom in Puerto Rico is to have a bridal doll covered with pins bearing the couple's name and wedding date. The pins are given to guests as favors. You might consider having smaller dolls adorned with pins on each table as centerpieces.

Russian: At Russian weddings, it is traditional for the newly married couple to give their guests gifts. Shop around for unique favors that you can give to your guests.

Scottish: In early days, a groom would purchase a silver spoon and have it engraved with the couple's initials and wedding date. You might want to buy yourselves a gift to commemorate your special day. The Scottish groom should consider wearing an heirloom kilt, and you might want to include bagpipe music in your wedding repetoire.

Spanish: In some regions of Spain, it was customary for a bride to wear a black silk dress and a mantilla adorned with orange blossoms. The groom would wear a shirt that his bride-to-be had embroidered.

Swedish: Attendants traditionally carried bouquets of strong fragrant herbs to ward off trolls, and the groom had thyme sewn into his clothes. Include fragrant blooms such as lavender or lilacs in your bouquets, or perhaps use bouquets of dried flowers and herbs.

Swiss: An old Swiss custom required a young attendant to carry a basket of colorful handkerchiefs. A guest could ''buy'' one by making a contribution to the couple's nest egg. Perhaps you would like to have a young attendant hand out colorful hankies monogrammed with your names and wedding date.

Vietnamese: Couples marrying in Vietnam traditionally have two celebrations: one given by the bride's parents and one by the groom's parents. Since red and pink are symbolic of happiness, consider using these colors in your attire, flowers, and decorations.

There is something special about incorporating cultural traditions into your wedding, and they can help to make your celebration unique. Talk to your relatives, clergy, a librarian or historian, or to members of cultural organizations to learn about ethnic customs that might be appropriate for your wedding.

❧ 6 ❧

Something Different— Alternative Weddings

BY NOW YOU'VE PROBABLY NOTICED A RECUR-
ring theme or message in this book—that this is *your*
wedding, and you should make every effort to have it
be the affair you want it to be. Some untraditional wedding settings have been mentioned in previous chapters,
and opting for something different can truly personalize
your wedding. Think about settings that are appealing
or special to you. The beach ... the mountains ... a
country inn or farm ... a boat? You might also consider
a museum, a castle, a historic house or estate, an arbo-
retum or botanical garden, a park, a rooftop garden, a
terrace or observation deck, a canyon, a ranch, or even
your college campus (maybe that's where you met).
With a little searching and investigation, you will be able
to get married in the place of your dreams. Call the local
chamber of commerce, municipal offices, or the department of parks and recreation for information on available locations as well as the logistics: fees, hours,
parking, and restrictions of any kind.

Home Sweet Home

In addition to the more unusual and highly personal wedding locations, there are some other types of weddings that you might want to consider. The first one is simple—a wedding at home. Whether it is your own home, or that of your parents or another relative or friend, this kind of wedding can be especially intimate and personal. Of course, it sounds simpler than it is in reality. If you are thinking about having a home wedding, consider your guest list. Can your house accommodate the number of guests you wish to invite? If not, are you amenable to paring down the list? It is important when planning a home wedding to have a skilled and reliable caterer and servers. Make sure that they are able to work in smaller kitchens, and that they can bring to the home all of the utensils and equipment they will need.

In order to insure that a home wedding runs smoothly, it is wise to ask certain people to take charge of specific tasks. For example, someone should be stationed at the door to greet guests and tell them where to go; maybe someone else takes the guests' coats and puts them in a designated room. Someone might be responsible for distributing wedding programs if you have them; someone else might be prepared to change the music if you are using a stereo. With a little organization and cooperation from those "designated helpers," a home wedding can be a beautiful affair.

The Great Outdoors

If you plan to have your wedding in the backyard, be prepared to move the party indoors if it rains. The same alternate plans must be made for any outdoor wedding. If you're planning a wedding in a park, state the alternate location (for example, the town hall) on the invitations. Even if you're getting married at a traditional wedding hall and plan an outdoor ceremony, make sure that the hall can accommodate last-minute weather changes. They must be prepared to set up indoors if need be.

Outdoor weddings can be traditional formal or informal affairs, or celebrations that are more unusual. How about a picnic wedding in the park? After the ceremony, willing guests can change into shorts and participate in the fun: volleyball, softball, dancing to taped music. You might serve a barbecue, watermelon, and cake, and favors could be baseball caps or miniature Frisbees with your names and the date printed on them!

A Candlelight Ceremony

A late afternoon or evening ceremony glittering with candlelight can be a most beautiful wedding. You can have candle stands placed at the end of each row of seats, and also on each side of the area where you will be standing. Your attendants can even carry candles in the processional. If you have teenaged relatives, you might ask them to do the honor of lighting the candles, or acolytes can do it for you. A "unity candle" is a beautiful symbol of your marriage. This is a single unlit candle that stands before you. At the appropriate moment in the ceremony, you each take a lit candle from the holders at your side and light the unity candle together.

Special Themes

Weddings with themes are unique and memorable events. You might want to have a period celebration (for example, Victorian or Colonial) complete with appropriate costumes, decorations, music, food, and entertainment. Can you picture a Renaissance wedding with jugglers and jousters, or a Mardi Gras celebration with a Cajun buffet? Some couples wish to express their cultures and heritages in all aspects of the wedding: clothing, music, food, and so on. If the couple are both sports enthusiasts, how about a wedding on the baseball diamond or the putting green? The reception could take place either on the grounds or in the club facilities.

Double the Fun!

Is your best friend planning a wedding too? Maybe you want to do it together. Not just the planning—have a double ceremony and reception! If two siblings are getting married at about the same time, having a double wedding can save a lot of hassle and cost. The invitations can be joint or sent separately. If the double wedding is to be a traditional affair, you'll want to coordinate the colors and style of attire. At the ceremony, the bridal parties usually enter one at a time. If the brides are sisters, the older one usually walks in first; or their father might escort them both together. The double ceremony will take a little thought and planning, and it should be an arrangement that is comfortable and mutually agreed upon by everyone.

A joint reception follows the ceremony. The bridal parties can sit together or separately, depending on the number of attendants. A double wedding might require a little extra planning—but it's double the fun!

Wedding in Uniform

Another unusual type of wedding that might be pertinent to you is a military wedding. Whether it's the bride or groom or both who are officers, they can marry in full-dress uniform or traditional formal attire. The couple's fellow officers form an arch of swords at the end of the ceremony, through which the newly married couple walks, adding a regal air to the wedding. You might decide to incorporate a patriotic theme throughout the reception by playing military marches, having a military band, using red, white, and blue floral arrangements, and featuring wedding favors with a patriotic motif. If you do plan a military wedding, consult with the appropriate personnel early on to insure that your plans coincide with the proper guidelines and requirements.

The Civil Ceremony

If you don't want to elope but are not interested in having a big wedding, you can be married by a county clerk, judge, or justice of the peace. The ceremony can take place at the courthouse or at the home or office of the officiator. You could have your parents present with you, or two honor attendants. After this quiet ceremony, you might want to have a luncheon, dinner, or party for family and friends.

A Weekend Wedding

If you have a lot of friends and relatives who are traveling to your wedding from different locations, you might want to make a weekend of it! If your wedding is on Sunday, plan a rehearsal on Friday, followed by dinner; invite some friends and cousins to join you for drinks or dessert afterward. Saturday can be spent doing various activities, such as a museum tour, a softball game, or whatever is appropriate. The wedding is on Sunday, and for those who are staying Sunday night, plan a brunch on Monday. After a leisurely morning, you can head off for your honeymoon!

When planning a weekend wedding, send guests a "wedding itinerary" in advance that outlines the weekend's events. Enlist the help of relatives or friends who can serve as contacts for guests should they have any questions prior to the big weekend. Provide maps and other tourist information in each guest's hotel room, along with a small welcoming gift. Finally, although the bride and groom should attend each event, they needn't stay the entire time.

Multiple Celebrations

If your families happen to live on opposite sides of the country—or your families are so spread out that no single location is convenient—consider having two weddings! You could have one small ceremony, and then parties in two different places. If you have friends and family scattered across the map, take some time off to travel to different places, visiting and celebrating. Keep a scrapbook or photo album that chronicles each visit, party, or event. Of course, only those with considerable energy and a high tolerance for stress should consider doing this. It can be exhausting, so give yourself ample time to plan—and do ask for help!

Wedding and Honeymoon in One

A trend that seems to be growing more popular is to have your wedding at your honeymoon site. This could mean a romantic marriage on a cruise through the Caribbean, or a wedding luau in Hawaii! Whatever your destination, be sure to check the legalities, such as whether you must be a resident in order to obtain a marriage license. Tourist bureaus and embassies can probably provide the necessary information and help you with your plans. How do you plan a honeymoon wedding? Ask the concierge of the hotel where you will stay to recommend a wedding consultant. Some hotels even host weddings of this sort themselves. As with any wedding, make sure that you obtain detailed written contracts for everything. Allow plenty of time for paperwork and overseas mail, and make sure that your home state recognizes out-of-state/country marriages.

Although you may not be able to share this honeymoon wedding with family and friends, it is a unique and personal way to get married and might be worth pursuing—if you're game! If a parent or anyone else is offended or upset by your plans, try to explain the best you can why this is important to you. Hopefully, everyone will understand. Ultimately, this is your wedding, and you should do it in the way that is most significant to you. You can always celebrate with others when you return home.

Personalizing Your Wedding

No matter where you decide to have your ceremony or what type of wedding you have, here are some unusual twists to help make your celebration unique:

- Switch positions with the official so that you and your wedding party are facing the guests.
- If your ceremony will be very small, have everyone gather around you during the ceremony.
- Walk down the aisle together.
- Include a cherished pet in your wedding party.
- Ask your guests to recite together a poem or prayer.
- Walk from the ceremony to the reception site if it is not too far.
- Release colorful—or elegant white, silver, or gold— helium balloons at the end of the ceremony.
- If you have a wedding program, include a note from you to your guests—either your thoughts on marriage or a thank-you.

7

Remarriages and Reaffirmations

CONSIDERING THAT THERE IS A 50 PERCENT DI-
vorce rate in this country, remarriages are a very common occurrence. There are several alternatives to consider when planning your remarriage, and your choices
will depend on your ages, whether you have children,
and whether this is a second marriage for one or for both
of you. You should not only decide what type of wedding you would like to have, but also take into consideration what will be acceptable to your close family and
friends.

Announcing Your Engagement

If you have children, they should be the first to hear
your good news. Depending on their ages and the nature
of your relationship, they may have suspected that a
marriage was inevitable. When you discuss your plans
with your children, you should stress the positive aspects
of your marrying and forming a new family together.
You want your children to feel as if they are acquiring
a new parent, not losing an old one. If your former
spouse is actively involved with the children, you should

notify him/her of your impending marriage.

Once you've told your children, you'll want to tell your parents, relatives, and friends. It is appropriate for you to announce your engagement in the newspapers, though if you are very recently widowed or divorced, you might want to skip the engagement announcement and simply publish a wedding announcement instead. If the bride is marrying for the first time, her parents may wish to make the engagement announcement. If she is remarrying, or if you have both been living independently for a while, you'll probably want to announce your own engagement (see Chapter 1).

Planning Your Ceremony

Contemporary remarriages can be of any style you wish, and yours should reflect your unique relationship. Many couples who are remarrying prefer a small ceremony followed by a large reception. In this way they can involve all of the people they want in their wedding celebration without offending relatives who feel that a lavish ceremony is inappropriate. Some couples like to plan a wedding very different from their previous ones. Others might choose to do most things in exactly the same way. The first thing you should do as you plan your wedding is to consult with the clergy member or official whom you want to perform the ceremony. Inquire about any restrictions or rules regarding remarriages of divorced people.

If you have children, you might want to involve them in the ceremony. Younger children can be either ring or flower bearers, while older children can read a prayer or poem. Consider having your children walk down the aisle or even stand at the altar with you. Including them in this way will make them feel that they are an integral part of your marriage and new family. If, however, your children do not want to participate, do respect their wishes. Try to be as understanding as possible about their concerns and fears. It may take time, but creating a new family from two existing ones is always a worthwhile and exciting endeavor.

Invitations and Announcements

If the bride is marrying for the first time and her parents are sponsoring the wedding, they may issue invitations in the customary way, as described in Chapter 13. When the bride and groom are sponsoring their own wedding, they can send their own invitations. A very small wedding does not necessitate formal printed invitations, but is suited by notes or telephone calls to invite guests. For larger affairs, you can send printed invitations that read like this:

> The honour of your presence
> is requested at the marriage of
> Nancy Smith
> to
> Howard Gill
> Saturday, the seventh of June
> at two o'clock
> The Waldorf Astoria
> New York

R.s.v.p.
521 Park Avenue
New York, New York 10023

If you are planning a large reception but a small ceremony, send printed invitations to the reception and include ceremony cards only for those guests who are invited to both events.

You may choose to send printed announcements after your wedding to let friends and colleagues know about your marriage. They can state that you are announcing your marriage, or that you are announcing the formation of your new family. For example:

Nancy Smith
and
Howard Gill
announce the formation of their
new family
Saturday, the seventh of June
One thousand nine hundred and ninety-two
New York

Your announcement could even be accompanied by a photograph of your new family.

Your Wedding Attire

In any wedding, whether a first marriage or a remarriage, you should wear the kind of attire that will make you feel special. The type of dress the bride chooses will depend on her age, the style of her wedding, and of course on what she and her husband feel is comfortable and appropriate. Many bridal stores carry gowns and dresses that are just right for remarriages. A bride who is remarrying should not feel prohibited from wearing white, as today the color symbolizes celebration. The groom will probably want to wear a tuxedo for a formal or semiformal wedding, or a dark suit for an informal affair. The bride's attendants can wear any type of dress you choose, but it should be similar in style and tone to your wedding attire.

Planning Your Reception

The reception for a remarriage can be of any style or size. You can follow the format and customs of a traditional reception, as described in Chapter 3, or you can forget all of the customary rituals and just have a big party. If you have children, do try to include them in the reception festivities as much as possible. Allow them to sit at the head table with you, dance with them, propose a toast to them and your new family, and perhaps give them gifts to commemorate the day.

The Wedding Budget

If this is a remarriage for both of you, you will probably sponsor your own wedding. It is up to you to decide how you will divide the costs, or if you will establish a joint "wedding fund" to pay for your affair. If it is the bride's first marriage, her parents can pay for the wedding if they are able to; the bride's parents might also accept the financial responsibility if the woman is a very young widow or divorcée, or if she is not financially independent. If both partners are remarrying but cannot afford to sponsor the wedding, either set of parents can offer to help them.

Your Honeymoon

As with any marriage—whether first, second, or third—a honeymoon is vital. It is important to get away and spend some time alone together, even if it just for a long weekend. If you have children, you might consider either taking them along or planning a two-part trip. If it's possible, get away by yourselves for a few days, and then take the kids on your first family vacation.

Reaffirming Your Wedding Vows

Reaffirmations have become popular today, particularly for those couples who eloped or were married in small civil ceremonies. In an age when lifelong marriages seem to be the exception rather than the rule, reaffirmation ceremonies are an important and beautiful way to celebrate the endurance of your own commitment.

Your reaffirmation ceremony can be a small intimate gathering, or a larger ceremony that includes friends and family both old and new. You can hold your reaffirmation in a church, hall, home, garden, or wherever best suits your tastes. If you have children, try to include them in the ceremony. You can either recite the vows you originally made to one another or write new ones that reflect the ways in which your relationship has changed and grown. You can celebrate after your reaffirmation ceremony with a dinner or party.

8

The Wedding Party

YOUR WEDDING PARTY SHOULD BE COM-
posed of the people you love and those who are closest
to you. Inviting those people to participate in your wedding is a very special thing, and they will feel honored
that you asked. Traditionally, the bride asks her sister(s),
sister(s)-in-law, and close female friends to stand up for
her, while the groom does the same with his brothers
and close male friends. However, if the bride has a close
male friend, her partner might include him among his
attendants. Conversely, the groom might have a close
female friend whom he would like to be included in the
wedding party. If you are willing to toss tradition aside
for your wedding, consider integrating the wedding party
to include both women and men as attendants for either
the bride or the groom.

The Bride and the Groom

The different members of the wedding party, including the bride and groom, traditionally have specific roles
and responsibilities, though these may vary depending
on the style of your wedding. More than ever before,
brides and grooms are planning their weddings together.
It is up to you to discuss your plans with your parents,

go over the budget and itemize estimated costs, and then start shopping for the services your wedding will require. It is your responsibility not only to plan the wedding you want, but also to take into consideration the needs and comfort of your guests as you plan.

As the bride you probably will want to shop for dresses with your attendants. Keep in mind the tastes of each woman, as well as her budget. The groom is responsible for informing his attendants of the men's attire you've chosen. Both of you should give your respective attendants gifts as a token of love and appreciation. The bride and groom can also hold separate parties, dinners, or luncheons for their attendants, or they may choose to go out together as a group to celebrate before the wedding.

Finally, the bride and groom are responsible for properly thanking guests for their gifts. You should write short, but personal, thank-you notes promptly.

Bride's Honor Attendant

The bride's honor attendant is the person responsible for helping the bride, not only on the big day, but with the preparations as well. Whether lending moral support or assisting the bride with her gown, the honor attendant should help in whatever ways are necessary. The honor attendant usually serves as a witness and signs the marriage certificate. During the ceremony, she holds the groom's ring and gives it to the bride at the appropriate moment.

The honor attendant's primary pre-wedding responsibility is throwing the bridal shower. This can be either a traditional ''women only'' shower, or a party honoring the couple together. The honor attendant should discuss the shower plans with the bride's mother and mother-in-law (or with all parents if it is to be a joint party) and with the other attendants. The responsibility for planning the shower can be divided among the attendants, and the cost can be shared too.

Some showers have a theme, such as kitchen, household, garden, gourmet, and so on. Others are more generalized. Since the couple may already have accumulated a lot of necessities—especially if they have been living together—it is a good idea for the honor attendant to ask the couple for a list of things they do need. Then, as people respond to the invitations, the honor attendant can suggest items on the 'wish list.' This will avoid the duplication of gifts. (See Chapter 9 for more on showers.)

Groom's Honor Attendant

The groom's honor attendant assists the groom in whatever ways necessary, including signing the marriage license, which he can safeguard along with the bride's ring. The honor attendant will most likely be the first person to propose a toast to you. If you are leaving for your honeymoon immediately after the reception, he might take responsibility for your baggage and other necessary items for your trip. He also could be the one to drive you to the airport or train station if necessary.

Just as the bride's honor attendant hosts the shower, the groom's honor attendant usually throws a bachelor party for the groom. Traditionally a raucous men's party, today the bachelor party can be something quite different. It might be a baseball game or other sporting event, an evening at a sports bar, or an overnight party at a cabin in the mountains. There are many possibilities—the bachelor party needn't be the stereotypical "one last fling" that it used to be. (See Chapter 9 for more on bachelor parties.)

Bridal Attendants and Ushers

The bridal attendants do not have specific pre-wedding duties, though they should be willing to help the bride with whatever she may need. After the ceremony or at the reception, they can stand in the receiving line or they can mingle with guests. The ushers' primary role is to seat guests as they arrive for the ceremony. Afterward, they should escort the mother, grandmothers, and other elderly or disabled guests to leave first. At the reception, the ushers mingle with guests and may propose toasts, too.

Children

Children can be an adorable addition to any wedding party. You might want to ask young nephews and nieces to be ring bearers, flower bearers, or junior attendants. If your gown has a long train, you might have pages, either boys or girls, hold it for you as you walk down the aisle. A candlelight ceremony could include a few older children or teenagers to light the candles.

Be sure to speak directly to the children or teenagers when you ask them to be in your wedding; don't go through their parents. This will convey your respect for them as well as the fact that they are important to you. If a child or teenager hesitates in accepting or refuses to participate, be understanding and let them know that it's okay to say no.

Because younger children's behavior is unpredictable, be prepared to have someone handle them if they should get restless or act out during the ceremony. As long as someone is nearby and ready to deal with the children in an emergency, all should go smoothly.

Pets

Finally, this may sound strange, but it has been done! As you gather your wedding party, don't forget your pet! If your cat or dog is an integral part of your lives, you needn't leave him out of your celebration. An outdoor wedding or one at home could easily accommodate a pet. If your dog or cat is agreeable, he/she can sport a bow tie, a wreath of flowers, or even a small box attached to a collar to hold your rings. Fluffy could even walk down the aisle!

❦ 9 ❧

Pre-Wedding Festivities

An Engagement Party

As a couple engaged to be married, you will probably be honored with several gatherings and parties before your big day. First, as mentioned earlier, you may want to have an engagement party. This could be an intimate dinner with family and friends, or you might want to throw a bigger bash. Rather than telling people about their engagement and then celebrating, some couples choose to announce their good news at a party they host.

Showers

Showers are parties that are not only fun, but functional too, since they help equip the couple for their new life together. Traditionally given by the bride's honor attendant, the shower today can be hosted by the attendants together, by friends of the couple, or by anyone who wishes to throw one. The shower needn't be an all-women affair given for the bride alone. Just as bachelor parties have changed over time, so too have showers. It is not uncommon these days for a shower to be given for the couple together.

Showers can be held at any time of day and be of any type. They are usually given a month or two before the wedding, before things get too hectic! Brunch has become a popular time for a shower. Typically, showers are informal and feature a light meal. Some showers even involve games that focus on the couple to be married. For example, the shower hosts can think up trivia questions about the bride and groom, or invent funny fill-in-the-blank sentences.

The hosts of the shower can invite guests by mail or by phone. Usually, only those invited to the wedding are invited to the shower, except of course, in the case of an office shower. Your coworkers may want to throw a party for you, though they won't necessarily expect to be invited to the wedding. If the shower is for you as a couple, only close relatives and friends invited to the wedding need be invited to the shower. If it is an all-women shower, the host needn't invite women who you don't really know or are not close to you (except for your fiancé's close relatives and friends, of course). Many showers are thrown as a surprise, but if you know that more than one is being planned for you, do try to combine the parties. If this is not feasible, at least try to make sure that there are no duplicates in the guest lists. You don't want a guest feeling obligated to give more than one shower gift!

It used to be that remarriages did not include showers. Today, however, showers are considered a fun and festive way to honor any couple about to be married. Since a couple remarrying will already have most of the necessities for their home, guests can chip in to give them a bigger gift, or give them more frivolous gifts. Guests might consider giving magazine subscriptions, liquor, gourmet food baskets, gift certificates to stores or restaurants, tickets to a show, or some other more unusual gifts.

Shower Themes

Many showers are given with a particular theme. If the host knows that the couple needs particular types of gifts, he/she might choose the theme accordingly. Following are some popular shower themes.

Lingerie showers: These may not be the most practical showers, but they certainly are fun! They also allow the bride to receive gifts that she might not necessarily purchase for herself. Nightwear, sexy panties and bras, and other intimate apparel are things that are enjoyable to give as well as to receive. Other personal gifts can include toiletries, perfume, jewelry, a picture frame or photo album—this is a really special gift if you can fill it with memorable pictures.

Kitchen showers: The kitchen theme is useful, particularly if the couple is setting up a new home. It is also a good theme for guests because it offers a wide range of gift options and prices: everything from dishes and flatware to small gadgets and cleaning supplies. A kitchen shower might also include favorite recipes. The host can ask each guest to purchase a gift that is necessary or relevant to the recipe she/he will offer. For example, someone offering a dessert recipe can give parfait glasses, too; a stir-fry recipe could be accompanied by a wok. The host can either supply each guest with a recipe card and then put them in a file box to present to the bride or couple; or a blank recipe book can be circulated in which each guest can inscribe their culinary treat.

Linen showers: These showers are also useful, both to couples setting up new homes and to those who have been living together and want or need new things. It seems as if you can never have enough bath towels, sheets, and dishtowels. Linen showers can also include tablecloths, place mats, cloth napkins and napkin rings, blankets, comforters, pillows, bedspreads, dust ruffles, shams, and bathroom accessories.

Gourmet showers: For those couples who love to cook—and eat—why not throw a gourmet shower? Gifts can range from cookware, to baskets of fancy foods and condiments, to gift certificates for restaurants or gourmet stores.

Other showers: If the bride and groom have particular hobbies—for example, they are outdoors enthusiasts—a shower reflecting the hobby theme could be fun. If the couple seems to have everything they need, a service shower might be appreciated. The guests each offer some service to the couple: doing yard work, helping to paint their home, cooking dinner for them, or any other task that needs to be done.

The Bachelor Party

The other big pre-wedding festivity is, of course, the bachelor party. This celebration can be a fun way for the groom to spend an evening with close friends, and to help ease his nerves, if necessary, before the big day. While some bachelor parties are of the traditional sort—the men only going to a burlesque show—it is becoming more popular to do other things, like go to a sports event or play a game of softball followed by a barbecue.

Traditionally, the groom's honor attendant organizes and hosts the bachelor party, though he might want to include the other attendants. Guests usually chip in to pay for the party, and they might bring small presents, often gag gifts. It's a good idea to have the bachelor party at least a week in advance of the wedding. Throwing it a night or two beforehand could cause the guys to be tired out for the big day!

The Bridal Attendants' Party

This pre-wedding tradition often seems to be by-passed, but if the bride has the time and is so inclined, it is a thoughtful gesture. She can treat her attendants to a brunch, luncheon, or even a dinner party to which they might bring spouses or dates. The attendants' party is a way for the bride to thank her attendants, and also for everyone to get acquainted before the wedding. The bride might also use it as an opportunity to confirm everyone's fittings and attire, as well as any other last-minute plans.

If you choose, instead of having a bridal attendants' party, you may want to host a party for all of your attendants. This would be a good occasion to present them with their gifts, and to thank them for sharing in all of your wedding preparations.

The Rehearsal Dinner

Most weddings include a rehearsal held a night or two beforehand, and usually followed by a dinner for the entire wedding party, the ceremony official, parents, and any other close relatives you would like to attend. The occasion can be as informal or as elegant as you would like it to be, and it can be held at a club or restaurant or at home. Consider toasting your parents at the rehearsal dinner, if it is appropriate, and you can also give your attendants their gifts if you haven't already done so.

Wedding Day Breakfast

If you would like, you can plan a breakfast the morning of your wedding. This is a thoughtful thing to do, particularly if you expect several out-of-town guests. You, your attendants, and your parents need not attend the breakfast since you will obviously be busy preparing for the wedding. Ask a relative or friend who would be willing to help organize the breakfast and play the role of host. Then, be sure to invite guests in advance, either by including a note in their invitations, or by calling or writing to them separately.

❧ 10 ❧

All Dressed Up

WHETHER YOU WERE "BORN TO SHOP" OR not, shopping for your wedding clothes and accessories will probably be one of the most enjoyable aspects of planning your wedding. Naturally, the style of your wedding and the season will help determine the kind of attire you will wear.

Bridal Attire

You should begin shopping for your bridal gown approximately six months in advance, if possible, since it can take three or four months for an ordered gown to be delivered. You will also want to shop as soon as possible if you are having your gown individually designed and sewn by a seamstress or tailor. Once you find your gown, you should shop for the attendants' gowns; or you can do it all at once, if you don't have many attendants and this is more convenient. Since renting the men's formalwear is relatively easy, shopping for styles can be done a few months in advance.

Bridal gowns come in an array of styles, and choosing the right one can be an overwhelming ordeal. Begin your search slowly. Don't go shopping for the first time and expect to return home with a gown. Just go with the goal of eliminating styles you do not like and narrowing down the choices. You might get lucky and find a gown that you know is the right one immediately. But don't get discouraged if you don't—there are plenty more stores and styles for you to explore.

It's a good idea to shop for your gown with someone who knows you well and knows your personal sense of style. If your mother wants to shop with you but you don't find her to be helpful, do your initial shopping with her, then explain that you want to make the final decision on your own, without anyone else's influence. You might want to bring along your honor attendant and/or a good friend on your shopping expedition, though keep in mind that too many people could make the process slow and confusing. If you have a very small bridal party, it might be most convenient and efficient for you to shop for all of the gowns and dresses together.

For a very formal wedding, you will probably want to wear a gown with a cathedral or chapel-length train. You also would wear a headpiece with a full-length veil, and perhaps gloves. For a formal wedding your gown could be slightly less elaborate, and would probably have a chapel or sweep train. Your headpiece could have a shoulder-length or fingertip veil, or you might want to wear a hat. Semiformal weddings traditionally call for a train-less floor-length gown or a dress. You might wear a hat or flowers in your hair, or a headpiece with a short veil. For an informal wedding, consider wearing an elegant suit or dress, and perhaps a hat or flowers in your hair.

Of course, you can always toss tradition to the wind! This is *your* wedding, and you should wear whatever is most comfortable and pleasing to you. If you are planning a backyard wedding, there's no law that says you can't dress in a formal gown and train. If you are in the military, by all means wear full-dress uniform if you want to. Then again, you might choose not to wear traditional wedding attire at all! If you are planning a period celebration, you most likely will wear an original or replica gown from that era. You're having a winter wedding? Why not wear luscious white velvet or a gown with fur trim? If your wedding will have a regional motif, make sure that your clothing does too! An ornate, beaded suede outfit would be perfect for a wedding with a Southwestern or Native American theme. Perhaps you want to play on cultural themes by wearing a silky kimono, a colorful sari, or any other appropriate native dress. You should be as elaborate or as untraditional as you want—as long as your attire makes you feel gorgeous and happy!

There are a variety of bridal gown styles and fabrics, and the following list of terms should help clarify them for you. Being familiar with these words will help you as you shop.

Fabrics

Brocade: a heavy fabric with a raised design.
Charmeuse: light, smooth silk or synthetic fabric.
Chiffon: usually silk or rayon material with either a soft or stiff finish.
Chintz: cotton fabric with floral patterns.
Eyelet: open-weave embroidery.
Faille: silk or rayon fabric that is slightly stiff.
Moire: silk taffeta that glistens in the light.
Organza: very sheer, crisp material.
Shantung: rough-textured silk or rayon fabric.
Silk-faced satin: full-bodied with a lustrous sheen.
Slipper satin: stiff satin made of acetate.
Taffeta: stiff fabric with small crosswise rib.
Tulle: fine, sheet netting of silk, rayon, or nylon.

Dress Styles

Ballgown: drop-shoulder bodice, natural waistline with full skirt.
Basque: natural waist with V-front.
Empire: short, scooped bodice with high waist and slender skirt.
Princess: slim-fitting with vertical seams from shoulders to hem.
Sheath: narrow, body-hugging dress with no waist.

Dress and Train Lengths

Street length: hem falls just below knees.
Intermission length: hem falls just below knee in front, reaches the ankle in back.
Ballet length: hem falls to center of calf or slightly lower.
Floor length: hem skims the floor.
Sweep train: train barely sweeps the floor.
Court train: one foot longer than sweep train.
Chapel train: approximately one-and-a-third yards long.
Cathedral train: very formal train, two-and-a-half yards long.

Train Styles

Attached train: falls from back end of skirt.
Detachable train: begins at waistline and can be removed.
Capelet train: falls from back of shoulder.
Watteau train: falls from back yoke.

Veils

Ballet length: falls to the ankles.

Blusher: loose veil worn over the face or back over the headpiece.

Birdcage: usually attached to a hat, it falls just below the chin.

Cathedral length: usually worn with a cathedral train, this veil is about three-and-a-half yards long.

Chapel length: approximately two-and-a-third yards long.

Fingertip: falls to the fingertips.

Fly-away: shoulder-length, multilayered veil.

Headpieces

Chignon: cluster of flowers attached to comb worn at back of head.

Floral wreath: wreath of fresh or silk flowers that can be worn on top of head or at mid-forehead.

Half wreath: covers half or less of head.

Half hat: covers half or less of back of head.

Juliet cap: ornate cap worn on back of head.

Mantilla: lace veil that frames the face.

Picture hat: large-brimmed ornate hat.

Profile: cluster of flowers attached to comb worn on one side of head.

Tiara: ornate crown worn on top of head.

Necklines

Boat: follows curve of collarbone and same line in back.

Drop shoulder: falls below the shoulder.

High: just touches the chin.

Queen Anne: high at back of neck, lower in front.

Square: squared off in front.

Sweetheart: shaped in front like the top of a heart.

Sleeves

Cap: small sleeve that just covers the shoulder and very top of the arm.
Dolman: very loose, large sleeves, often fitted at wrists.
Leg-of-Mutton: wide and round at shoulder, snug fit on lower arm.
Melon: large and round from shoulder to elbow.
Puff: short, round sleeve.
Three-Quarter: ends between the elbow and wrist.

Where to Shop

There are several options for buying or renting a bridal gown or dress, and you should investigate to determine which best suits your needs and budget. Traditional bridal shops offer a full range of bridal and attendant gowns as well as dresses for mothers. They will not only help you select a gown and headpiece, but will provide (at additional cost, of course) the proper lingerie: bra, petticoat, slip, stockings, garter. Bridal stores usually have seamstresses and tailors on site, and they will arrange fittings. The cost of bridal attire purchased from a specialty shop usually begins at approximately $800 and rises according to the designer and manufacturer of the gown you choose.

If you've been perusing bridal magazines, you may have spotted gowns that you like by specific manufacturers. You can look for them in bridal shops, or contact the manufacturer to find out if they have an outlet or showroom in your vicinity. If you live in a large city, there may be bridal showrooms that carry attire by various manufacturers. Although it can be impersonal and overwhelming to shop in a showroom, you can get some good buys on designer gowns. You should also contact local department stores to find out if they run sales on bridal gowns. For example, Filenes of Boston holds an annual bridal sale, when they sell designer gowns at very low prices. Again, the experience of shopping at a sale of this kind can be harrowing, but it may be the way for you to get the gown you want—at the price you can afford!

If you have a particular style and look in mind and want something entirely unique, you might have a seamstress or tailor design and make your gown. This can be very costly, unless of course you know someone who will give you a break! But the result is that you will wear a one-of-a-kind gown or dress.

A popular alternative to buying a new gown or dress is to wear an heirloom. Does your mother or grandmother still have her gown? If it is in decent condition, it might be very special to wear it. Or, if it is not in good shape, you might be able to salvage some lace that could be added either to your own gown or headpiece or to your bouquet. Would you consider wearing your sister's gown? Some women don't want to get married in a gown that has been worn by another bride, but there is something special about wearing a "family gown" and perhaps preserving it for your own daughter.

If you don't have an heirloom gown in the family, but do like the antique look, you might want to shop at vintage clothing stores. Wearing an antique gown or dress reflects a sense of history at a time when you are embarking on a new future. An antique bridal gown combined with vintage-look attendants' dresses can make for a delicate and beautiful Victorian wedding.

Used bridal gowns may not sound attractive or elegant, but the reality is that they can look just as attractive and elegant as a new gown, and cost a whole lot less! Even though another bride has worn the gown, once you put it on, it becomes all yours.

Another option is not to buy a gown or dress at all. Rent one! This is fast becoming a viable alternative for women who cannot afford the high cost of bridal attire, or who choose not to spend the money on a gown, but on another aspect of the wedding. Gowns and dresses for brides and attendants are available through rental shops. If you consider that your bridal gown may sit forever in your attic—or that the fancy dresses you want for your attendants are expensive and probably not wearable again—renting doesn't seem like such a bad idea. If you can get past the psychological notion against wearing something "used," renting attire may be just the right option for you!

Topping It All Off

You've got your gown—what to wear on your head? Hats are nice for daytime or outdoor weddings. They can be small caps or wide-brimmed, depending on your taste, and they may have veils attached to them. Before you choose a headpiece, think about how you want to wear your hair. If you have long hair that you want to pile on top of your head, a hat might not be practical. Instead, a beaded headband with a veil might work better. When you shop for your gown and headpiece, it's a good idea to style your hair in the way you will wear it for your wedding. That will give you the best idea of the overall look of your outfit.

If you are a traditionalist, don't forget: "Something old, something new, something borrowed, something blue—and a penny in your shoe!" Following the rhyme, which began in Elizabethan England, guarantees a life of good luck. Something old could be an heirloom gown or jewelry; something new could also be your gown, or shoes or lingerie. You might want to borrow a handkerchief, jewelry, or a purse, and your lingerie or a garter can be adorned with a ribbon of blue. The penny in your shoe is supposed to insure prosperity.

Preserving Your Gown

You may want to have your gown preserved after the wedding. A professional dry cleaner can do it by cleaning, wrapping, and sealing the gown in an airtight box. You can also preserve your gown yourself. After having it dry-cleaned, fold the dress with layers of acid-free tissue (your dry cleaner can suggest where to buy it), then wrap it in unbleached muslin. Store the dress in a cedar chest or wooden drawer in a cool, dry place. Never store the gown on a hanger or in a plastic garment bag, as this will not allow the dress to breathe. Air it out periodically and fold it slightly differently before storing it again. Preserving your gown makes it usable for future generations, or perhaps for you to wear again if you ever have a reaffirmation ceremony.

Attendants' Dresses

Finding the right attendants' dresses or gowns can be more difficult than finding a bridal gown, since there may be several different sizes, shapes, and tastes to accommodate. Generally, the attendants' gowns should have a degree of formality and elegance similar to your bridal gown. Usually, the honor attendant wears a different but complementary style and/or color to set her apart from the other attendants. If you only have two attendants, however, you might prefer that they wear the same dress. Again, the attendants' attire is up to you, though you should consider colors and styles that will complement all of the women.

Many brides try to select dresses that the attendants can wear again for formal dinners or parties. If you will have several attendants in your bridal party, you might allow the women to wear similar dresses but in different colors. For instance, for a semiformal autumn wedding, you might have your attendants wear simple velvet floor-length dresses in maroon, forest green, midnight blue, and royal purple. Although the colors are different, they are all deep, rich hues that blend together.

Another option is to select a basic style of dress and allow each attendant to alter it subtly to suit her individual taste. For example, you are planning a spring wedding and have chosen a salmon-pink attendant's dress. It is a simple, floor-length gown of cotton-polyester with a slight sheen to the fabric. Perhaps your honor attendant prefers a V-neck, slightly off the shoulder, lined with small pearls. One of your attendants might want a rounded neck, cap sleeves, and a narrow sash at the waist. Another attendant looks best with a drop shoulder and piping that forms a V at the waist. Yet another attendant might want a square neckline and cinched waist. Although each dress is slightly different, the styles especially complement each woman's figure, and the overall effect is stunning.

If you like a contemporary look—and your attendants want to be able to dance up a storm—shop for dresses that have detachable skirts. Some dresses actually come in two pieces: a short dress—perhaps made of lace over silk—with a full, ballet-length taffeta skirt worn over the dress. After the ceremony and picture taking, your attendants can remove their skirts and kick up their heels in their short lace dresses. This look is all contemporary elegance—and it's practical too!

Shoes and Accessories

You and your attendants should be sure to choose shoes that are comfortable. Low heels are probably best, especially if you like to dance. The style of your dresses will determine whether you choose satin-look shoes or those ornamented with lace or beads. Most women prefer to have everyone's shoes dyed to match the color of their dresses. Usually the store where the shoes are bought can dye them; all you need to do is provide a small swatch of material from your dress.

Your attendants can wear headpieces, flowers, or nothing at all in their hair. Your florist or a bridal shop can make barrettes or combs with flowers that the women can use if they have long hair. They might prefer to wear fancy beaded headbands. Jewelry is optional for both the bride and her attendants. Often the attire is so elaborate that simple stud or pearl earrings and perhaps a necklace or bracelet are all you need. If it is appropriate, the bride might choose, as her gift to them, to buy her attendants jewelry that they can wear with their dresses.

Men's Formalwear

The groom's attire should complement the bride's clothing and be appropriate for the season, time of day, and style of the wedding. Very formal daytime weddings usually feature the groom and groomsmen in black or gray cutaway coats with solid or striped pants, and formal white shirts. Very formal evening weddings usually call for a black tailcoat, black slacks, and a wing-collared shirt with French cuffs. For a formal wedding, groom and groomsmen can wear black or gray stroller jackets, or for formal evening weddings, black tie—a black or charcoal tuxedo and pleated white shirt. The men can wear suits with white shirts and matching ties for semiformal or informal weddings.

The men's accessories include cummerbunds, vests, suspenders, ascots or ties, cuff links, shirt studs, and perhaps gloves for very formal affairs. The following list describes various formalwear elements and styles. It helps to be familiar with the terms before you begin shopping.

White tie: The most formal, this consists of a black tail-coat, matching trousers, a white piqué vest and tie, and a white winged-collar shirt with piqué front.

Tuxedo: Formal evening wear, this is a black or gray jacket with a shawl, peak or notch lapels in satin or grosgrain; worn with matching slacks and a white winged-collar shirt.

Cutaway or morning coat: Formal day wear in black or gray with striped pants, a winged-collar shirt, and ascot.

Stroller: This jacket is cut slightly longer than a suit jacket. It is black or gray and worn with striped pants, a white lay-down shirt, and a four-in-hand tie.

Winged-collar: A stand-up band collar with folded down tips; may have pleats.

Lay-down collar: Similar to a business shirt.

Ascot: Double-knot tie folded over and worn with a stickpin.

Four-in-hand tie: Similar to a regular tie.

Studs: Worn instead of buttons on a formal shirt.

Cummerbund: A wide sash that covers the waist of slacks.

You can collect brochures from various formalwear shops to help you select the style and color of tuxedos and accessories. As with the women's attire, you should choose the formalwear you like best and that which you will be most comfortable wearing. If you are planning a very formal evening wedding but think you will feel self-conscious in a tailcoat because you are short, don't wear one! On the other hand, if you are having a day wedding but want to wear a tailcoat, go for it! Try on a variety of styles and choose whatever feels right for you.

For a military wedding, the groom and/or bride should wear full-dress uniform, as should any attendants who are in the military. If you want to emphasize your heritage at your wedding, the groom might consider wearing his national attire. For example, families of Scottish descent often have a clan tartan which the groom can wear with a formal jacket.

The groom usually differentiates himself from the other men by wearing different accessories. For instance, he might wear a black cummerbund and tie, while the ushers wear cummerbunds and ties in another color. Often the groom also wears a different boutonniere, as can the best man, in order to set him apart. You might consider, for instance, having the groom wear a boutonniere of three roses, his honor attendant one of two roses, and the ushers one of a single rose.

Parents' Attire

As with the bridal party attire, the mothers of the bride and groom should dress according to the style of the wedding. They will probably want to wear floor-length dresses for very formal affairs, and either floor-length or shorter dresses for formal weddings, depending on the time of day. Usually the mothers coordinate styles and colors, not only with each other, but with the attendants as well. Traditionally, the bride's mother chooses her outfit first, and the groom's mother coordinates with hers. Today, however, wedding planning is becoming more and more collaborative. Your mothers may simply discuss their tastes beforehand—or maybe they'd like to shop together! The fathers of the bride and groom usually dress to match the groom's attendants, either wearing tuxedos or suits.

Children's Clothing

If you are planning to have children in your wedding party, dressing them up can be lots of fun! Velvet dresses or tiny floral prints look adorable on flower girls. Your ring bearer would look sweet in a velvet suit, a tiny tuxedo, or jacket and shorts. When choosing the children's clothes, do consider their comfort too. A child who is comfortable is more likely to be better behaved!

Your Rings

Now you're all dressed up . . . but what about the rings? Shopping for wedding bands is exciting and fun. If you are looking for plain bands or traditional styles, you can shop at any jewelry store and compare quality and prices. If you want a unique ring, seek out individual jewelers and artisan galleries that showcase jewelry. Perhaps you'd like to design your own bands and have them made by a jeweler. No matter what kind of rings you decide to buy, they will forever be a personalized symbol of your love and union.

Clothing Chart

Bridal Gown
   Store:
   Address:
   Phone:
   Contact:
   Manufacturer/Style No.:
   Description:

   Price: Delivery Date:
   Fittings: _____   _____   _____

Headpiece
   Style No.:
   Description:

   Price: Delivery Date:

All Dressed Up

Attendants' Dresses:
  Store:
  Address:
  Phone:
  Contact:
  Manufacturer/Style No.:
  Description:

Price: Delivery Date:

Headpieces:
  Style No.:
  Description:

Price: Delivery Date:

Accessories/Prices:

Men's Formalwear:
  Store:
  Address:
  Phone:
  Contact:
  Designer/Style No.:
  Description—Groom's:

Description—Ushers:

Price: Pickup Date/Time:
Fittings: _____   _____   _____

Money-Saving Tips

- Instead of a bridal gown, purchase a fancy white dress.
- Look for sales, discontinued styles, sample dresses.

The Wedding Planner

- Shop at department stores instead of bridal shops.
- Shop from bridal catalogues or rental stores.
- Buy dresses and shoes that can be worn again.
- Make your own garter, ring pillow, bridal purse.

❧ 11 ❧

"Say Cheese!"

Finding a Photographer

Choosing an excellent photographer—and perhaps videographer—is extremely important. After all, this is the person responsible for providing you with a lifelong pictorial memory of your wedding day. Take the time to shop around for a photographer, and ask friends or relatives for recommendations.

Large photography studios often employ several photographers. When you look through sample albums or portfolios, note the names of the photographers you are interested in and ask whether these people are available on your date. Your contract with the studio should specify the photographer's name; if it doesn't, the studio is not obliged to send any particular photographer, and that means you might end up with someone other than who you chose.

Photography studios are not your only option. There are excellent photographers who work independently, often out of their own homes. This does not mean that they are any less professional or talented. What it does mean is less overhead cost for them, and therefore lower expense for you. It could also mean that they have more time to devote to each individual wedding, as opposed to what an overbooked studio might be able to offer.

The Wedding Planner

Choosing a Videographer

In addition to still photographs, you might decide to capture your wedding on video. Videotapes of your wedding can be straightforward, unedited tapes, or they can be finely edited movies with music and captions. Some are so elaborate they chronicle special moments of your lives leading up to the wedding as well. When you shop for a videographer, ask to see samples of his/her work. You should inquire about equipment and ask to view the lighting the videographer will use. Most modern lights are not as blinding as older video equipment. You should decide how you want to format your video, including captions and music, and how elaborate you want it to be. Also specify to the videographer whether or not you want all of the guests to express personal greetings on the tape, or whether there are just certain people that you want the videographer to approach. You should make clear to the videographer just how "intrusive" you want her/him to be.

If you don't feel you need a formal or professional videotape, you might consider asking a friend or relative to tape your wedding. You can buy or rent a video camera, or the person you ask may have one already. An amateur video can be just as enjoyable to watch in years to come as a professional one—and a lot less costly too!

Selecting the Shots

As you shop for a photographer, you should think about the kinds of shots you want to have taken. Most photographers have standard shots and packages that they offer, but if you want something additional or different, ask ahead of time if the photographer can accommodate you. Don't forget to include the specifics in the contract.

You'll want your photographer to strike a nice balance

between posed shots and candids. If you choose, you can have a wedding portrait—either of the bride alone or the bride and groom together—taken before the wedding. This is usually the shot that is sent to newspapers along with the wedding announcement. Some couples choose to take their formal bridal party shots between the ceremony and the reception. Others have them taken immediately before the ceremony, or even several days in advance. Although it detracts from the element of surprise on the big day, photographing in advance does allow you to enjoy your reception without interruptions.

Your photographer will take formal pictures of you and your bridal party, and your parents and families. He or she will also photograph each person in the processional, the ceremony itself if this is allowed, and the recessional. If you are getting married in a church or synagogue, you should consult with the clergy about requirements. Some will not allow flash photography during a mass or during the ceremony.

At the reception, your photographer will shoot your "entrance", your first dance, dances with your parents, the bridal table, the cake and cake cutting, the best man as he toasts you, any individuals who sing or otherwise entertain or toast you, as well as formal shots of each table. Make sure that your photographer also gets lots of candid shots of everyone dancing and having a good time.

Several guests may bring their own cameras, or you might want to purchase disposable cameras to place on each table for guests to use. Most likely they will get great shots that your photographer misses. If there is someone special who can not attend your wedding, ask someone present to take Polaroid pictures which can be sent or taken to that person soon after the event. Seeing the candid pictures right away will help ease that person's disappointment at not being able to share your special day.

The Wedding Planner

The Photography Contract

The photography "package" usually includes an 8 × 10 portrait, several 5 × 7 portraits, your album, two parents albums, and perhaps wallet-size pictures if you want to include them in your thank-you cards. If you do not want the wallet-size pictures, ask if you can substitute something for them—perhaps extra 5 × 7 shots or more pictures in your album. You should inquire whether the proofs are included or if there is an extra charge to keep them.

Your contract with the photographer should list by size all of the pictures you will get; it should specify the number of pages and/or pictures in each album, whether proofs are included or an extra cost, the number of hours the photographer will work, overtime cost, the date the proofs will be ready, and perhaps most important, the name of the photographer! The following chart will help you keep your photography options organized.

Photography Chart

Photographer's name:
Studio:
Address:
Phone:
Photographer's hours:
Bridal album/No. of pages:
Parents albums/No. of pages:
No. of proofs?   Extra charge to keep them?

No. of: 8 × 10
          5 × 7
          wallet-size
Date proofs ready:
Total cost: Deposit: Balance due:

"Say Cheese!"

Photos We Want

Bridal portrait
Bridal suite pictures
Bride and groom with each set of parents
Bride with parents
Groom with parents
Processional
Recessional
During ceremony
Receiving line
Bride with grandparents
Groom with grandparents
Bridal party
Bride with honor attendant
Groom with honor attendant
Separate attendants
Bride and groom's first dance
Dancing with parents
Parents dancing
Attendants dancing
Guests dancing
Family portraits
Individual table shots
Cake cutting
Bouquet/Garter toss
Honor attendant's toast
Other:

Videotape Chart

Videographer's name:
Address:
Phone:
Hours of work:

The Wedding Planner

Length of tape:
Description:

Special effects/sound:

Cost: Deposit: Balance due:
Additional tapes/cost:
Date ready:

Money-Saving Tips

- Have the photographer take select formal shots only;
  fill out your album with candids taken by guests.
- Ask a shutterbug friend to photograph or videotape
  your wedding.
- Evaluate photo packages carefully; don't choose one
  that offers a lot of things you do not want; do ask if
  you can make substitutions in the package to get what
  you want.

And the Band Played On

MUSIC WILL ADD A FESTIVE ATMOSPHERE TO your wedding reception and will help create a personal and special mood for your ceremony. There is a range of options when it comes to music, from the type of musicians you hire to the selections they will play. Give yourself plenty of time to think about the kind of music to suit the style of your wedding, and to listen to and choose selections.

Music for the Ceremony

If you are getting married in a church or chapel, you will most likely hire the church organist and perhaps the choir. Your clergy or the house musicians can probably suggest appropriate selections for your ceremony, which includes the processional, the recessional, and any music you want to have during the ceremony itself. Religious councils and groups might also be able to suggest musical selections for you to use. Once you've gotten ideas from your clergy, books, or other sources, spend some time listening to music. You can go to a library that has a ''listening room'', or check out albums and listen to them at home.

Ask the organist, choir, or cantor if you can hear a

performance of a variety of selections; then choose those you like best. If you have other numbers in mind, tell the musicians well in advance so that they have ample time to practice. No matter what denomination or faith, if you are marrying in a house of worship, do consult with the clergy regarding the ceremony music. Some do not allow popular tunes—even if they are mellow renditions—but require classical music.

You may prefer not to use the house organist, choir, or cantor, but to hire outside musicians. You might have a friend who is a vocalist and wants to sing a solo. Again, check to make sure that your plans are acceptable to your clergy. Think about the kind of music that would best suit the setting for your ceremony. Do you hear a string quartet, or a woodwind ensemble? A band of trumpeters, or a harp player? A lute or mandolin player, a flute and guitar duet, or a pianist? You can always hire professional musicians, but to save on your budget, consider hiring high school or college students, or asking any musical relatives or friends to perform. If hiring musicians is not an option for you, taped music can be just as effective and enjoyable.

Music for the Reception

The musical options for your reception are just as varied as those for your ceremony, and again, the style and tone will help you select the music. If you are having an outdoor reception, you might want a string quartet or woodwind ensemble to play throughout. Or perhaps you'd like a swing band with a wooden dance floor set up. If you hire musicians to play during the ceremony, consider having them provide the cocktail hour music as well. Then the band or a DJ can pick up as the dining and dancing begin.

Think carefully about how you want the music orchestrated during the reception. Do you want the band or DJ to play more or less continuously throughout, or do you want the bandleader or DJ to tell guests when each course is being served? Do you want mellow music played during the meal, or nothing at all?

You might have a negative reaction to the mention of polkas, waltzes, or ethnic dances, but remember your guests. There may be some who will *only* dance to these tunes or to slow songs. You may think that the hokey-pokey, the electric slide, and other group dances are silly, but they usually do serve to get even the most inhibited dancers up on their feet. Make clear to the band or DJ the kinds of music you want and the variety, and be sure that this is stated in your contract.

There are highlights of your reception for which you might want to choose special music. For instance, your first dance, the bride's dance with her father, and the cake cutting. If you do not specify the music you want, the musicians or DJ will play traditional tunes (for example, during the cake cutting, the band usually sings, "The bride cuts the cake" to the tune of "The Farmer in the Dell").

As you audition bands, musicians, or DJs, ask what they include in their repertoire. Make sure that it consists of a solid variety of music, and if you have special requests, tell the musicians well in advance so that they have ample time to learn and practice them. Like photography studios, musical entertainment groups often have several musicians that they assign to different "gigs." Your contract should specify the names of the musicians in your band—and these should be the ones you auditioned. Your contract should also specify the kinds of music you want, the hours the band will play, the band's attire, and whether or not band members will be fed at the reception.

If hiring a band is beyond your budget, consider hiring a DJ to orchestrate the music. DJs usually come equipped with their own music and equipment, and you can also collect music for the DJ to use. You might just want to rent audio equipment and play your own tapes. Perhaps you have a friend who is a musical mix-master who will help you make tapes—and maybe be in charge of the music at your wedding! As with musicians, a less expensive alternative to hiring a professional DJ is to hire a high school or college student, or someone else you know who does this as a hobby or profession.

Whatever kind of music you choose, take the time to think about what you and your guests would like to listen and dance to. The right music can really help make your wedding the most pleasurable and fun that it can be!

Music Selections

Here is a list of some classical music you might consider for the prelude to the ceremony, the processional, recessional, or the ceremony itself.

- Bridal Chorus from *Lohengrin* (''Here Comes the Bride'') by Wagner
- ''Wedding March'' by Mendelssohn
- ''Water Music'' by Handel
- ''Trumpet Voluntary'' by Clarke
- Canon in D minor by Pachelbel
- ''Sarabande'' from Suite No. 11 by Handel
- ''Spring'' from *The Four Seasons* by Vivaldi
- ''Fanfare'' from *The Triumphant* by Couperin
- ''Ave Maria'' by Schubert
- ''First Organ Sonata'' by Mendelssohn
- ''Hallelujah Chorus'' from *The Messiah* by Handel
- ''Ode to Joy'' by Beethoven
- ''Jesu, Joy of Man's Desiring'' by Bach
- ''Trumpet Tune'' by Purcell
- ''Apotheosis'' from *Sleeping Beauty* by Tchaikovsky

And the Band Played On

Here are some contemporary selections for you to consider for the ceremony or the reception:

- "Benedictus" by Simon and Garfunkel
- "The First Time" by Roberta Flack
- "Wedding Song" by Stookey
- "You Are So Beautiful" by Joe Cocker
- "Longer" by Dan Fogelberg
- "Lady" by Kenny Rogers
- "You Light Up My Life" by Debby Boone
- "We've Only Just Begun" by The Carpenters
- "I Love You Just the Way You Are" by Billy Joel
- "Time in a Bottle" by Jim Croce
- "Through the Eyes of Love" by Sager/Hamlisch
- "I'll Always Love You" by Taylor Dayne
- "You Are the Sunshine of My Life" by Stevie Wonder
- "Endless Love" by Diana Ross/Lionel Ritchie
- "Saving All My Love for You" by Whitney Houston
- "Just You and I" by Melissa Manchester
- "The Wind Beneath My Wings" by Bette Midler
- "Evergreen" by Barbra Streisand
- "Unforgettable" by Natalie Cole
- "On the Wings of Love" by Jeffrey Osborne
- "Annie's Song" by John Denver

Musicians

Band name:
Phone:
Contact:
Type of music:
Hours needed:
Musicians' names:
Cost:
Notes:

The Wedding Planner

Our Music Selections

Use this chart to fill in the pieces you have chosen for each aspect of your wedding:

Ceremony:
> Introduction:
> Processional:
> During ceremony:
> Recessional:

Reception:
> Receiving line/cocktail hour:
> First dance:
> Dances with parents:
> Dances with bridal party:
> Dinner music:
> Cake cutting:
> Ethnic dances:
> Group dances:
> Other:

Money-Saving Tips

- Hire a DJ instead of a live band.
- Use your own tapes and ask someone to be in charge of changing the music.
- Hire music students instead of professional musicians.
- Ask musical friends or relatives to contribute their talents.

❧ 13 ❧

Flowers Say It All

FLOWERS BURSTING WITH COLOR AND LIFE—A beautiful way to enhance any wedding! No matter where you're getting married or what kind of wedding you are planning, you'll probably want to adorn your celebration with the natural beauty of plants and flowers.

Flowers for the Ceremony

If your ceremony is in a house of worship, you might want to decorate the altar with sprays of flowers, and perhaps mark the ends of the pews with small ribboned bouquets. If you plan a Jewish ceremony, consider decorating the *huppah* with flowers and ivy vines. If you are marrying at your reception site, it is probably most important to decorate the area for the ceremony with dramatic bouquets. A white latticed partition erected behind the officiator can be intertwined with ivy and blossoms.

Even if your ceremony is outdoors, you may need to add more color and decoration with flowers. If you'll be standing in a gazebo, this can be beautifully garnished with flowers. You might also use some potted plants to border the ceremony area, perhaps lining the path you will walk down.

A good florist will be able to help you decide the

amount of floral decorations you will need for your ceremony, as well as the kinds of flowers to use. The availability of certain plants and flowers during different seasons is a factor to consider, though even if a flower is out of season, it can usually be ordered from another region of the country.

For a spring wedding, consider using cherry blossoms or branches of yellow forsythia, Easter lilies, tulips, jonquils, daffodils, geraniums, and violets. Roses, stephanotis, peonies, snapdragons, daisies, gladioli, and forget-me-nots, just to name a few, are lovely summer blooms. If your wedding will be in autumn, you might want to use chrysanthemums, spider mums, asters, dahlias, and orchids. You might also consider using dried flowers, either alone or mixed with fresh flowers. For a winter wedding, you can choose from roses, carnations, holly, poinsettias, and of course, any other flowers or plants that your florist is able to order.

The style of your wedding as well as the setting will help determine the types of floral arrangments and decorations that you should have. For instance, a contemporary wedding might call for sparse but dramatic arrangements, while a Victorian wedding could use fresh or dried flowers. A very spacious church will require larger arrangements, whereas a ceremony in an intimate chapel would be overpowered by these kinds of sprays and would probably look better with smaller, simpler bouquets and potted plants.

Flowers for the Reception

Flowers can make an ordinary reception hall a stunning and personalized place. The size of the room, the number of tables, and the style of your wedding will determine the types of table centerpieces you should have. You may opt for very lavish centerpieces, but if the number of tables in the room makes them overpowering, consider alternating them with candle centerpieces that have a simple ring of flowers around the base. In addition to the centerpieces, you might also want to have an arrangement on the place-card table, flowers on the cake table, and perhaps standing bouquets or potted green plants or trees around the band area.

The Language of Flowers

Flowers have been given certain meanings over time. Here are some common flowers used in weddings and their traditional ''meanings'':

Roses	Love
Violets	Fidelity
Gardenias	Joy
Orchids	Beauty
Lilies	Purity
Daisies	Innocence
Carnations	Distinction
Daffodils	Regard
Honeysuckle	Affection
Jasmine	Amiability
Camellia	Beauty
Orange blossoms	Fertility
Forget-Me-Nots	Love
Lily of the valley	Happiness

You might want to consult books on flowers in your local library to find out the symbolic meanings attributed to various blossoms. Your florist may also have information that describes the ''language'' of flowers.

All of these things—season, style, the language of flowers—can help you decide what kind of flowers you want. But if it seems difficult to envision the bouquets and arrangements your florist describes, don't worry too much about it. Your florist is a professional who probably has plenty of experience decorating weddings. Although you should ask to see samples of your florist's work and consult with her/him regarding the decorations and arrangements, you can probably rest assured that your florist will know just the way to add beauty and flair to your wedding.

Bouquets, Corsages, and Boutonnieres

Besides the centerpieces and floral decorations for your ceremony and reception, you need to choose flowers for the bouquets, corsages, and boutonnieres. Again, your florist should be able to design an attractive bouquet that compliments your gown. You'll need to describe yours and your attendants' attire in detail, or give your florist a picture if possible. The florist will take into consideration factors such as the style of the gowns or dresses, the height of the women, as well as the season and style of your wedding. If you want to personalize your attendants' bouquets, consider including their favorite flower or birth-month flower. Your florist will also design the attendants' headpieces, and your own if you plan to wear a wreath of flowers. The headpiece flowers can be either fresh or silk. A tip when choosing the attendants' flowers: ask everyone in your bridal party if they are allergic to any particular plants or flowers!

Your florist will be able to suggest types of flowers that work well and hold up in boutonnieres. You'll also need to describe the men's formalwear so that the florist can take this into consideration. Sometimes the honor attendants have a different boutonniere and bouquet. This is probably not necessary if there are only two attendants on each side, but the decision is up to you.

You will also need to order corsages for your mothers and grandmothers. A trend or "floral style" that is pop-

ular is to give each mother and grandmother a single
flower to carry, for instance a long-stemmed rose. It is
also nice to honor other participants in your wedding
with flowers. If your aunt is going to say a blessing
before the meal, or if your cousin will sing a solo at
your ceremony, it would be thoughtful to show your
appreciation by giving them corsages or single flowers.

Preserving Your Wedding Flowers

Finally, if you plan to toss your bridal bouquet at your
reception, but you feel you just won't be able to let it
go, have your florist make a separate bouquet! It can be
either a replica of yours or just a small nosegay. Your
florist can preserve your bouquet and boutonniere for
you or tell you how to do it yourself; or you can dry
the flowers and make a potpourri, or press them in a
book. If you have your vows written and framed, you
can use the pressed flowers to decorate it; or you can
arrange a few pressed buds under the glass covering
your framed bridal portrait. Perhaps you'd like to com-
pile an album or scrapbook with your invitation, pressed
flowers, candid pictures, and other mementos of your
special day. Use your imagination and you can probably
think of some way to keep your wedding flowers your
whole life long.

Flowers Chart

Florist:
Address:
Phone:
Contact:

Ceremony:
  Description of flowers:
  Price: Delivery time:

The Wedding Planner

Reception:
   No. of centerpieces: Price each:
   Description:
   Cake table:

   Price:
   Buffet table:

   Price:
   Other:

Bouquets/Boutonnieres:

Bridal Bouquet:
   Price:

Throw-Away Bouquet:
   Price:

Attendants' Bouquets:
   Number: Price each:

Boutonnieres:
   Groom:
   Best man:
   Ushers:
   Fathers:
   Number: Price each:

Corsages:
   Mothers:
   Grandmothers:
   Other:
   Number: Price each:

Headpieces:
   Price:

Money-Saving Tips

- If another couple is getting married on your date at your ceremony site, share the cost of floral decorations.
- Choose floral decorations that can be used for both the ceremony and reception.
- Flowers in season are less expensive than those that must be ordered.
- Instead of corsages or attendants' bouquets, have each woman carry a single bud or flower.

❦ 14 ❧

Spreading the News

YOU'VE SPENT DAYS, WEEKS, MONTHS PLAN-
ning THE perfect wedding. Now it's time to invite people to it! Your invitations should reflect the style of your
affair. Formal weddings would be well suited by ivory
paper with black ink, and traditional wording of the invitation. An informal wedding, on the other hand, might
call for an invitation with an embossed design, and perhaps colored ink. For a very small wedding, it would be
appropriate to send personal notes rather than printed
invitations. If you are planning an untraditional wedding,
invitations that reflect the nature of the event will indicate this to your guests and help put them in the right
frame of mind for whatever is in store!

Forming the Guest List

You and your parents have probably been jotting
down names of people you would like to invite. Once
you have all composed your guest ''wish lists,'' you'll
probably want to sit down together, if possible, to com-
pile a master list. Unfortunately, wish lists have a way
of growing longer and longer, and your budget may not
allow so many people. If this is the case, you'll need to
pare down your guest list; but don't toss away the names

you have cut! Invariably, you will receive some regrets, and you then may be able to invite others from the original list. You've probably heard of the ''A List/B List'' phenomenon. Some people even have a C List! Your friends and relatives should not be insulted if they receive a late invitation and assume they were on the B List. They should realize that you'd invite everyone if you could, but that's just not realistic.

You should also bear in mind that it is acceptable to invite more people to the ceremony than to the reception. If your ceremony will be held in a big enough space, and if you have friends or coworkers you would like to share in your wedding but cannot invite to the reception, by all means invite them to the ceremony. Most people understand the difficulty of forming a guest list when, as in most cases, finances are limited. Inviting people to the ceremony only is a nice way of compromising—it makes guests feel as though they have been considered, and it allows you to share your special day with as many people as possible.

Once you've composed the guest list, it may be useful for you to begin either an index card file, a notebook, or a computer log that contains the name, address, and phone number of each guest, as well as whether he/she is invited to the ceremony, reception, or both. Once you begin to receive responses, you can mark the appropriate card or entry in your log to indicate whether that person will attend. You can also use the log or file cards to indicate whether a guest has special dietary needs, as well as to record gifts. This may seem obsessive to you, but it is an efficient and organized way to keep track of your guests, especially if you are planning a large wedding.

Shopping for Invitations

You can shop for invitations at stationers, printing shops, and fine gift and craft stores. Usually, these shops have binders that contain a wide variety of invitations. Although you may have a particular style in mind, peruse the books anyway. You might just find something you like better! If you are artistic, perhaps you'd like to design your own invitations, or you might ask an artistic friend to do it.

The Words to Say It

Once you have selected the invitation, you'll have to choose the typeface you want as well as the color of ink. Most important, you'll need to decide on the wording of your invitation. Traditionally, if the bride's family is hosting the wedding, the invitation would state that they are inviting the guests to the affair. For example:

Harold and Susan Bickford
request the honor of your presence
at the marriage of their daughter
Sarah
to
Jeffrey Taggert
Sunday, the tenth of October
at half-past eleven
St. Luke's Church
San Francisco

The reception card for this traditional formal invitation would read:

Reception
immediately following the ceremony
The Regency Hotel
San Francisco
Kindly Respond

If you want the invitations to include the groom's parents, there are two options:

Spreading the News

Harold and Susan Bickford
request the pleasure of your company
at the marriage of their daughter
Sarah
to
Jeffrey Taggert
son of
Walter and Sheila Taggert
etc.

Or:

Harold and Susan Bickford
and
Walter and Sheila Taggert
request the pleasure of your company
at the marriage of their children
Sarah Bickford
and
Jeffrey Taggert
etc.

If one or both of you is a professional, you can include your title or degree along with your name. For instance:

Harold and Susan Bickford
and
Walter and Sheila Taggert
request the pleasure of your company
at the marriage of their children
Doctor Sarah Bickford
and
Jeffrey Taggert
etc.

108

If you are hosting your own wedding, your invitations could read:

> The honour of your presence
> is requested at the marriage of
> Sarah Bickford
> to
> Jeffrey Taggert
> *etc.*

Couples who are having double ring weddings can send invitations together or separately, depending on their preferences. A joint invitation could read:

> Frederick and Nina Hall
> and
> George and Mary Snyder
> request the honor of your presence
> at the marriage of their daughter
> Elizabeth Ann Hall
> to
> Timothy John Remson
> and
> Kathleen Susan Snyder
> to
> Matthew Peter MacLeod
> *etc.*

If you are planning a military wedding, the invitations should include service titles. If an officer holds the rank of captain or higher in the Army, Air Force, or Marine Corps, or senior lieutenant or higher in the Navy, the title preceeds the name. For example:

> Edward and Beth Samuelson
> request the honor of your presence

Spreading the News

at the marriage of their daughter
Captain Mary Samuelson
United States Army
to
Mark Anthony Brown
etc.

Usually noncommissioned officers, privates in the Army, Air Force, and Marine Corps, and junior or petty officers in the Navy state their name followed by their title and the service branch. For example:

Thomas Avery
Ensign, United States Navy

If the bride or groom is in the Reserves in active service, the correct wording is "Army of the United States," or "United States Naval Reserve," instead of United States Army or United States Navy. If the bride or groom is a military student, the title "Cadet" is used under the appropriate name, followed by the service branch.

The above examples use traditional phrasing, but you should feel free to word your invitations in whatever way you see fit. As long as your invitations reflect the style of your wedding, contain all of the necessary information, and are easy to follow, you can be as creative as you want to be!

A more personal tone to the wording of traditional invitations is becoming popular. One example:

Stephen and Paula Greene
and
George and Alison DeSantos
invite you
to share in the joy

of the marriage
uniting their children
Sharon and Richard
at St. Ann's Church
Hawthorne, New Jersey
Sunday, the twentieth of June
at half-past eleven.
Join us afterward at
Mayfair Farms
West Orange, New Jersey

If all of your guests are invited to both the ceremony and reception, you could indicate both on one invitation. If you are sending more invitations to the ceremony than to the reception, you'll need to include a reception card to those who are invited to the reception as well.

Invitation Enclosures

Your invitations can include an address to which guests are requested to respond, and you can ask for a response using "R.S.V.P.," "Please Respond," "Kindly Respond," or "The favor of a reply is requested." If you prefer, you can enclose response cards with your invitations. The return envelopes for these cards should be addressed and stamped. A simple response card reads:

_____ will _____ attend.

Rain cards are a must if you are planning an outdoor wedding. They should simply state where and when the wedding will be held in the event of rain.

If you intend to keep your maiden or professional name, or if you plan to hyphenate both names, you might want to include a *name card* with your invitations.

Spreading the News

These cards can also be sent to business and other associates who are not invited to the wedding, but whom you wish to inform. A name card would read:

Lisa Davis and William Reid
wish to announce that they will be
using the surname Davis-Reid
following their marriage
May 24, 1987

At-home cards are a convenient way to inform people of your new address. They can also simultaneously tell people what surname you will be using, thereby eliminating the need for name cards. For example:

Lisa and William Reid
—or—
Ms. Lisa Davis
and
Mr. William Reid
after the twenty-fourth of May
1230 Park Street
Oakland, California 90213

Finally, in addition to these various cards, it is a good idea to enclose with your invitations *directions* to both the ceremony and the reception.

Addressing and Assembling the Invitations

There is a proper way to address and assemble the invitations. The outer envelope should be addressed in full, without using state abbreviations. Proper titles, such as Doctor, Reverend, and Captain should be written out, although Mr., Mrs., and Ms. are abbreviated.

The inner envelope is unsealed, and should be addressed with last names only, as well as any children who are included. Children over the age of sixteen should receive a separate invitation. For example:

Mr. and Mrs. Johnson
or:

Ms. Tisch and Mr. Smith
or:

Mr. and Mrs. Johnson
or:

Paul and Elizabeth

When you invite a single person and want to give them the option of bringing a guest, it is appropriate to address the inner envelope to that person ''and Guest.'' If you know the guest, a separate invitation should be sent.

The invitation should be inserted into the inner envelope with the words facing up. Extra enclosures should be placed in the inner envelope, on top of the engraved side of the invitation, or inside the invitation if it is folded. Do not seal the inner envelope. Insert it into the outer envelope with the addressed side up. When people open the envelopes they should see their names as they pull out the inner envelopes.

Wedding Announcements

Wedding announcements are often sent to people who are not invited to the wedding, but whom you would like to inform of your marriage. The announcements can be sent by your parents or by yourselves, and should be mailed on the day or day after your ceremony. A typical announcement would read:

> Stephen and Paula Greene
> have the honor of announcing
> the marriage of their daughter
> Sharon
> to
> Richard DeSantos
> on Sunday, the twentieth of June
> 1992
> West Orange, New Jersey

Postponement or Cancellation

If you must postpone or cancel your wedding and invitations have already been sent, you should send cards to this effect as soon as possible. If you are postponing the wedding due to illness or death in the family, but have not set a new date, the card could read:

> Stephen and Paula Greene
> regret that a death in the family
> obliges them to recall the invitations
> to the wedding of their daughter
> Sunday, the twentieth of June

If you have chosen a new date, the card can announce that the wedding has been postponed from one date to another. Be sure to include the location again. If you are canceling your wedding, you should send cards stating simply that the wedding will not take place.

Other Stationery Items

In addition to invitations and the various other enclosures you may want, you will also need to order thank-you cards. These can be the same style as your invitations, or you might prefer some other stationery, perhaps with your names and address engraved on it. Your stationer or printer should have lots of options from which you can choose.

Don't forget other printed mementos, such as napkins or matchbooks, which you might want to ask your printer to do. Some couples also like to have wedding programs printed, particularly if they are having a long ceremony or if it involves several readings or songs. A program allows everyone to follow along with the readings, and it is a nice way to credit those who actively participate in your ceremony. If you have written your own vows, you might want to include them in the program too. Your printer can prepare your program professionally, but if you are skilled on a personal computer, you might want to create your own!

Stationery Chart

Store:
Phone:
Contact:

Invitations:
  Number:
  Description:
  Cost:

Reception Cards:
  Number:
  Cost:

Rain Cards:
  Number:
  Cost:

Response Cards:
  Number:
  Cost:

Name Cards:
  Number:
  Cost:

At-Home Cards:
  Number:
  Cost:

Announcements:
  Number:
  Description:
  Cost:

Thank-You Cards:
  Number:
  Description:

  Cost:

Other:
  Napkins
  Matchbooks
  Seating place cards
  Wedding progams

  TOTAL COST:

Money-Saving Tips

· Use mail ordered or prepackaged cards, or if you're
  artistic, make your own!

- Consider the weight of the invitation—the heavier it is, the more postage you'll pay.
- Compose wedding programs yourself (or have a friend do them) on a personal computer.
- Explore printing options with your stationer—some are cheaper than others.

❦ 15 ❧

Have Your Cake and Eat It Too

GOOD FOOD IS AN ESSENTIAL ELEMENT OF any gathering or occasion. If you are having your wedding at home, in a church or hall, or some other place where food is not provided, you will need to shop for a caterer. If your reception will take place at a location that does provide the food, you will need to plan the menu.

Choosing the Food

Before you do this, ask if you can sample various dishes. Some reception sites host open houses at which prospective customers can get a taste of the food as well as other decorative ideas for their weddings. You might want to consider whether any of your guests have special dietary needs, such as no-salt, low cholesterol, diabetic, vegetarian, kosher, food allergies, and so on, and make certain that your reception site can accommodate them.

If you are having a full meal and your reception site provides the food, you will usually begin with a cocktail hour and an open bar. The cocktail hour generally includes passed hors d'oeuvres as well as a table with a selection of carved meats, chafing dishes, fruit, cheese, and other goodies. The meal usually includes an appetizer, salad, the main course, and dessert. Most people like to offer two choices for the entrée, although this isn't necessary. Your reception site probably will have a variety of scrumptious desserts to choose from, or they may offer the sinful Viennese table—a smorgasbord of sweets to satisfy any palate!

Finally, the pièce de résistance: the wedding cake! Reception sites that provide food can usually provide a cake too, and often they give you a choice of several kinds: chocolate, bananas and strawberries, custard—whatever is your pleasure! Of course, if you want something truly unique—or if you know a great baker—you might want to order your cake separately from the other food. You can top your cake with the traditional bride and groom figures, or you can adorn it with fresh or silk flowers. There are also crystal and porcelain cake tops available, although these can be costly, so do shop around. In addition to the wedding cake, you might also want a "groom's cake," a dark fruitcake that can be cut up and boxed for guests to take home. The legend of the groom's cake says that a woman who puts a piece under her pillow will dream of the man she will marry!

If you are planning an untraditional wedding—a cocktail party, afternoon tea, or brunch—you naturally will plan your menu accordingly. You might consider including ethnic dishes, either as hors d'oeuvres or appetizers, or with the main course. If you are of different nationalitites, sharing cultural food could be an enjoyable experience for your guests. Another idea that makes for interesting eating is to feature during the cocktail hour several stations offering different ethnic foods: Chinese, Italian, Jewish deli foods, and so on.

Have Your Cake and Eat It Too

Finding a Caterer

If your reception site does not provide food, you'll need to shop for a good caterer. Perhaps the best way to find one is by word of mouth. Ask relatives, friends, and coworkers if they have any recommendations, and then explore these options first. This will be a much more efficient and productive way to find a good caterer than by starting a cold search.

When you consult with caterers, discuss not only what you would like to serve, but also the limitations of your budget. The caterer will be able to tell you what kind of meal, sit-down or buffet, for instance, would work best within your budget. Again, ask if you can sample some of the caterer's dishes. You should also ask the caterers you interview about the preparation and delivery of food, as well as the service of waiters and waitresses: Are they included or do they require an additional charge? Does the caterer provide the serving equipment, or will you need to supply any? Are china, glasses and flatware, and table linens included, or will you need to obtain these necessities separately? Does the caterer make the wedding cake, or will you need to find a baker too?

Depending on where your reception is to be held, you may need to rent tables, chairs, tents, a portable wooden dance floor, and so on. You'll need to inform the caterer about the kitchen facilities, and ask the caterer to visit the site ahead of time so that she/he is familiar with the kitchen.

The following charts will help you organize your food and beverage plans to insure that all of your guests will have their palates and bellies satisfied. *Bon appétit!*

Caterer

Name:
Address:

The Wedding Planner

Phone:

Price per person: Gratuities: Total:

Beverage Prices:
  Soft drinks:
  Coffee/Tea:

SERVICES: INCLUDED   EXTRA COST

  Waiters

  Bartenders

  China

  Glassware

  Flatware

  Linens

  Serving equipment

Your Wedding Cake

Bakery:
Address:
Phone:

Wedding Cake:
  Description:

Order By:
Delivery or pickup?   Time:
Price:

Groom's Cake:
  Description:

  Price:

  Notes:

Liquor

If you are hiring a caterer, you'll need to provide liquor and beverages, as well as bartenders, separately. A liquor wholesaler would probably be less expensive than a retail store, and can probably provide mixers along with the brands of liquor you may want. Most liquor dealers will accept returns on unopened bottles and charge only for the bottles used. This chart will help you organize the chore of choosing liquors. Your dealer can assist you in the selection while keeping within your budget. Consider having a wine- and champagne-tasting party for family and friends to help you choose the ones you want!

Liquor Store:
Address:
Phone:
Contact:

The Wedding Planner

LIQUOR	NO. OF BOTTLES	PRICE
_____		
_____		
_____		
_____		
_____		
_____		
_____		
_____		
_____		
_____		

Total cost:
Order by:
Delivery or pickup?   Time:

Champagne/Wine:
 Kind:
 Cost per case:
 No. of cases:
 Total cost:

Money-Saving Tips

- Enlist the culinary talents of friends and family to help make food.
- Culinary/baking schools often provide their services at the cost of the food only.

Have Your Cake and Eat It Too

- Borrow linens, dishes, glassware, serving equipment, and so on, instead of renting.
- Serve wine, beer, and a champagne punch instead of hard liquors.
- Compare the cost of providing liquor and beverages yourself, instead of having the caterer do so.

❧ 16 ❧

Just the Right Gift

Wedding Gift Registries

Although you may not think it is necessary to register at a store for gifts, you should consider this option carefully. Registries not only help guests select gifts, but also insure that you receive the things you want or need. Guests will feel that their money is being spent wisely, and registering will help avoid duplicate gifts. If you would like to acquire china, silver, and crystal, registering your patterns would be most advantageous and helpful in completing your service.

When and Where to Register

Begin assembling your gift "wish list" early, preferably soon after your engagement party, since you will probably receive gifts then. Decide what you need and then shop around for the kinds of items you want or the manufacturers you prefer, as well as the best store for you to register with.

Most department and china stores offer free registries that are computerized. This enables people to shop at any of the store's locations, which is a big consideration if you have any out-of-town guests. You can register at more than one store, though it is wise to register for different items at each store in order to avoid duplication.

Gifts to Register

You can use the following shopping list to record what you want, the number of each item you want, as well as how many you have received. The store you register at will probably have a consultant who can help you choose your gifts. The store may also offer appliance demonstrations and shows that might be helpful. Don't forget to inquire about any upcoming sales too. Be sure to register for gifts in different price ranges; less expensive items are appropriate as shower gifts, whereas larger items allow a few people to purchase a gift together if they choose. When your registry list is complete, do let friends and relatives know, and ask them to spread the word!

Exchanging or Returning Gifts

If you receive duplicate gifts or something that you really do not like or need, you can exchange or return the item at the store from which it was purchased. Bring it back in the box it came in and with the tags attached; you most likely will not have a problem returning or exchanging it. If a gift arrives damaged, inform the store, if possible, rather than the sender. The gift should be replaced without a problem. When you exchange a gift, you may tell the giver if you feel comfortable doing so. In your thank-you note, simply tell the guest that the gift was a duplicate, or that it didn't quite match your decor (whatever is a relevant reason). Then explain that you exchanged the gift for some other item (name the item), and thank them for their thoughtfulness and generosity. If you do not feel comfortable doing this, you should just send a thank-you card for the gift without mentioning the exchange or return.

Gift Registry

	NUMBER NEEDED	RECEIVED

Formal Dinnerware
Store:
Manufacturer:
Pattern:
  Dinner plates
  Lunch plates
  Dessert/Salad plates
  Bread/Butter plates
  Soup bowls
  Fruit bowls
  Coffee cups/saucers
  Teacups/saucers
  Demitasse/saucers
  Teapot
  Coffeepot
  Sugar/creamer
  Salt/Pepper shakers
  Serving bowls
  Serving platters
  Gravy boat
  Egg cups
  Other:

	NUMBER NEEDED	RECEIVED

Formal Flatware
Store:
Manufacturer:
Pattern:

Just the Right Gift

Dinner forks
Salad/Dessert forks
Cocktail forks
Tablespoons
Soup spoons
Teaspoons
Demitasse spoons
Long-handled spoons
Dinner knives
Steak knives
Butter knife
Sugar spoon/tongs
Lemon forks
Serving spoons
Serving forks
Gravy ladle
Cake knife
Pie server
Silver chest
Other:

	NUMBER NEEDED	RECEIVED

Serving Pieces
Store:
Coffee service
Tea service
Water pitcher
Champagne/Wine cooler
Serving platters
Serving bowls
Trays
Salad set
Utility knives
Tureens
Chafing dishes
Condiment dishes

Cream/Sugar set
Salt/Pepper shakers
Gravy boat
Dessert dishes
Candlesticks
Napkin Rings
Other:

NUMBER NEEDED   RECEIVED

Crystal
Store:
Manufacturer:
Pattern:
   Water goblets
   Wineglasses
   Champagne flutes
   Cocktail glasses
   Brandy snifters
   Shot glasses
   Liqueur glasses
   Beer glasses
   Iced Tea glasses
   Other:

Informal Dinnerware
Store:
Manufacturer:
Pattern:
   Dinner plates
   Salad plates
   Soup/Cereal bowls
   Dessert bowls
   Cups/saucers
   Mugs
   Serving plates
   Serving bowls
   Other:

	NUMBER NEEDED	RECEIVED

Informal Flatware
Store:
Manufacturer:
Pattern:
  Place settings
  Serving pieces
  Other:

Informal Glassware
Store:
Manufacturer:
Pattern:
  Water goblets
  Wineglasses
  Cocktail glasses
  Juice glasses
  Beer mugs
  Other:

	NUMBER NEEDED	RECEIVED

Bar Accessories
Store:
  Ice bucket
  Wine rack
  Coasters
  Jigger/tools
  Corkscrew/bottle opener
  Punch set
  Decanters
  Other:

Kitchen Items
Store:
  Food processor
  Coffeemaker

The Wedding Planner

NUMBER NEEDED   RECEIVED

Coffee grinder
Juice maker
Blender
Mixer
Toaster/toaster oven
Microwave oven
Deep fryer
Electric frying pan
Pressure cooker
Dutch oven
Microwave cookware
Large pots
Small pots
Sauce pots
Large frying pans
Small frying pans
Baking pans:
   Round
   Loaf
   Rectangular
   Square
   Spring pan
Wok
Fondue set
Mixing bowls
Hot plate
Teakettle
Canisters
Spice rack
Storage containers
Cutting boards
Utensils
Napkin holder
Other:

Just the Right Gift

Linens
Store:
    Formal tablecloths
    Formal napkins
    Informal tablecloths
    Informal napkins
    Place mats
    Potholders
    Dish towels
    Aprons
    Blankets
    Comforters
    Pillows
    Sheet sets
    Electric blanket
    Bath towels/washcloths
    Beach towels
    Bath mats
    Rug/lid sets
    Accessories:
        Wastebaskets
        Tissue holders
        Cups
        Soap dishes
Other:

NUMBER NEEDED   RECEIVED

Electronics
Store:
    Television
    VCR
    Stereo
    Camera
    Telephone

The Wedding Planner

Calculator
Other:

Household Items
Store:
  Lamps
  Clocks
  Vases
  Area rugs
  Fireplace accessories
  Decorative bookends
  Wall hangings/pictures
  TV/Computer table
  Other:

Miscellaneous
Store:
  Luggage
  Camping equipment
  Barbecue grill
  Outdoor furniture
  Exercise/Sporting equipment
  Pool/Beach items
  Tools
  Vacuum cleaner
  Hand-held vacuum
  Snack tables
  Folding table/chairs
  Other:

❦ 17 ❧

Getting to the Church
on Time

OR TO THE SYNAGOGUE, THE RECEPTION hall, the park, the historic estate, the mountain lodge—wherever you are getting married!

You can go the traditional limousine route, or you can choose another mode of transportation that is suitable to your wedding. A horse-drawn carriage would be lovely for a Victorian wedding. Vintage cars are another elegant way to travel. Of course, if you are planning a more outrageous wedding, be as creative as you want to be: horses, roller blades, motorcycles . . . whatever suits your fancy!

If your ceremony and reception are in different locations, you'll need to arrange for the transportation to wait until the ceremony is over and then take you to the reception. If you will have a photo session between the ceremony and the reception, at a separate location, don't forget to confirm that with the transportation as well. It is helpful to make a list or chart for each driver of the people who need to be picked up at what time. You can use the one at the end of this chapter, or devise your own.

Usually, the transportation is responsible only for getting the wedding party and families to the wedding. Make sure that everyone who arrives by the wedding transportation has a means of getting home!

A wedding which includes the ceremony and reception at the same site may not require transportation for the wedding party, but you might consider arranging transportation for out-of-town guests who will be arriving at airports or train stations. If you have several guests staying at a hotel, you might want to arrange for a hotel van or cabs to bring them to the wedding. If you are having a small wedding at an unusual location, you could hire a bus to take everyone to the wedding. Your guests could even begin the festivities early by having champagne and listening to music on the bus!

Transportation

Transportation company:
Address:
Phone:
Cost:

Driver:

PERSON	ADDRESS	PICK-UP TIME
_____		
_____		
_____		
_____		
_____		
_____		

Getting to the Church on Time

Bus Company:
Phone:
Cost:

PEOPLE: PICKUP TIME:

_____

_____

_____

_____

_____

_____

Cab Company:
Phone:
No. of Cabs:
Cost:

PEOPLE: PICKUP TIME:

_____

_____

_____

_____

_____

_____

The Wedding Planner

Money-Saving Tips

- Hire one or two limousines (for bride and attendants or the two families) and ask attendants to drive their own cars.
- Investigate options: Corporate limos are usually less expensive than luxury limos.
- Walk to the ceremony or reception, if possible—you can have a wedding parade!

❧ 18 ❧

Honeymoon Bliss

YOUR WEDDING DAY PROBABLY WILL BE THE fastest day of your life—it will go by so quickly, in fact, that you may want to do it all over again! Despite the tensions, arguments, and chaos of the wedding preparations, the end result always seems worth it.

But once your wedding is over, you will probably feel ready to take some time out for yourselves, to get away from it all and begin your married life together in a fresh, enjoyable way. Don't underestimate the importance of the honeymoon trip. It is the first time you will be together as a married couple, and what better way to begin but alone together, without the intrusions of everyday life. If you cannot take a vacation immediately following your wedding, do try to plan one as soon as possible afterward. It is valuable time to rest, relax, and most of all to spend quality time alone together.

Start planning your honeymoon early, and take time to decide what you want to do. It's probably best to plan a relaxing vacation that doesn't have the potential for too much stress. You will most likely have had enough of that already! But if you are an adventurous and easygoing couple, by all means go for whatever is most exciting for you.

Whether it is backpacking in the mountains, lying on

a beach, or traveling abroad, plan as much of the trip as necessary to make it comfortable and relaxing. Some couples like to plan every last detail of their vacations, while others are content to take off only with airplane tickets and baggage in hand. Traveling without an itinerary can make for spontaneous fun, but you have to do it with an open and flexible mind. If you tend to get uptight or feel unsettled when traveling, it's probably a good idea to plan your accommodations and itinerary in advance.

A good travel agent can help you plan the honeymoon of your dreams. Consult with several travel agents if you have to, in order to get firsthand information about the places you might want to go. Wherever you decide to travel, be sure to inquire about the weather, any national or international events that may be held during the time you will be there, the best means of traveling once you are there, whether you will need passports, visas, inoculations, and the like, the average price of accommodations, whether there is anything you should not eat or drink, and so on.

Remember to bring a camera on your trip—even a small disposable camera will do if you don't want to lug around a 35mm. Even if you don't enjoy taking pictures, or if you are not fond of shopping for souvenirs, remember that years from now you might wish you had some memorabilia from your wedding trip. Maybe you would like to collect labels from the bottles of wine you share; perhaps pick up business cards from the shops, restaurants, or other places you visit. Save your plane, train, or boat tickets as well as schedules or maps. All of these things can be used to make a fun scrapbook or album that chronicles your trip.

As relaxing and pleasurable as vacations can be, bear in mind that they do carry potential for stress and disappointment too. Your flight might be delayed; you might miss your train if you get stuck in traffic; your accommodations might turn out to be awful; you might lose your luggage; you could even become ill on your trip. But whatever happens, remember that it's just a vacation, and try to go with the flow. Although you might be full of expectations that your honeymoon will—and must—be the perfect trip, don't forget that you will have a lifetime of vacations together. Relax, be flexible and prepared to handle any rough spots, compromise along the way, and ENJOY IT!

Your Honeymoon

Things you may need:
    Passport
    Visa
    Inoculations
    Traveler's checks

Airline Information:

Train Information:

Accommodations:
    Hotel:
    Address:
    Phone:
    From: To:
    Cost:

Hotel:
Address:
Phone:
From: To:
Cost:

Money-Saving Tips

- Cruises and packaged tours can be more cost effective—explore your options thoroughly.
- Consider off-season traveling (for example, the Caribbean in summer or Europe in the winter).
- Book air travel and accommodations as far in advance as possible to take advantage of special promotions.
- Some travel agencies have wedding registries that enable guests to contribute a gift to your honeymoon trip.
- Don't keep your honeymoon a secret from a cruise ship captain or hotel concierge. Sometimes they will throw in a complimentary gift if they know you are newlyweds!

30-Day Countdown

YOU'RE DOWN TO THE LAST FEW WEEKS BE-
fore the big day. All of the major plans are set in place,
and you're probably hearing from guests and going for
your final fittings. You may think everything is taken
care of, but there always seem to be a few details that
have slipped through the cracks.

The Marriage License

This may sound silly and obvious, but don't forget
your marriage license! It's a simple detail, but you can't
get married without it! The requirements for a marriage
license may vary by state, so you should call your local
municipal offices to ask them the following questions:
(1) Who needs to sign it? If you need a witness, bring
along your best man or woman. (2) Are there age requirements? (3) Are there residence requirements? (4) Is
a blood test or doctor's report necessary? (5) What is
the fee? (6) Do you need to bring any legal documents,
such as a birth certificate? (7) Is there a waiting period
after the license is obtained?

Business Affairs

You've probably discussed things like finances and insurance. If you haven't already done so, now is the time to adjust your bank accounts, if necessary, and change the names on bank accounts and insurance policies, pension plans, stocks and bonds, and your will.

This leads to the question of names. Do you wish to change your name, or will you use both names and hyphenate them? Do you feel it is necessary to change your name at all? Many women who are known by their own names professionally desire to keep them for business purposes, and use their husband's names in their personal life. This, however, can get very confusing. Ultimately, you should do whatever feels most comfortable and appropriate for both of you.

If you do change your name, in addition to bank accounts and insurance policies, be sure to alter your driver's license, vehicle registration, property titles or leases, credit cards, voter registration, passports, subscriptions, club memberships, and any other necessary legal documents. Don't forget to tell the post office too! You might also want to notify colleagues, organizations to which you belong, and even family and friends. You can do this easily by sending name cards ordered through your printer or stationer.

While You're Away

Think about whether there is anything that needs to be done while you are on your honeymoon. How will your pets and plants be cared for? Do you want anyone to check on your home while you're gone? Have you stopped delivery of mail and newspapers? What about your wedding gifts? If you don't have time to visit the bank before leaving, fill out a deposit slip and ask a trusted friend or relative to deposit money for you. Will you have a chance to bring other gifts to your home, or should you ask someone else to take charge of keeping them until you return? If you expect to receive gifts of great value, you might want to get a temporary floater insurance policy in advance to cover them.

Confirming Services

Even though all of the wedding preparations may have been arranged for months, it is a good idea to confirm the various services a few weeks before the big day. Check with your ceremony and reception sites, your clergy or ceremony official, florist, caterer, baker, photographer, videographer, transportation, formalwear stores, rental stores, bridal shop, and any other services you have retained. If your florist is not delivering the flowers directly, you'll need to arrange who will take the various arrangements, corsages, and bouquets to the ceremony and reception sites, and what time they need to arrive. You should also confirm your travel plans, including transportation and accommodations.

Newspaper Announcements

Some couples like to submit a wedding announcement to their hometown newspapers. Usually, announcements are published the day after the event, and stories should be sent to the society editor at least ten days in advance. Call your newspaper to find out their deadlines and whether they have a standard form for you to complete. If your newspaper does not have a standard form, type your announcement double-spaced, and include your name, address, and phone number on it. If the paper will accept a photograph, send a black-and-white print of your bridal portrait with identification on the back. Check your local newspaper for examples of wedding announcements. This will give you an idea of how much information to include. An example of an announcement is as follows:

> Susan Smith, daughter of Matthew and Laura Smith, of Chicago, was married yesterday to Mr. Timothy O'Neal, son of James and Eileen O'Neal of Chicago. Msgr. Patrick McGrath performed the ceremony at Annunciation Church in Chicago.
>
> The bride, escorted by her parents, wore an ivory gown trimmed with lace and a picture hat. She carried a bouquet of calla lilies and rosebuds.
>
> Ms. Elissa Brady, the bride's cousin, was honor attendant. The bride's attendants were Lori Smith and Tracy O'Neal.
>
> Mr. Michael Ferry served as the groom's honor attendant. The ushers were Jerry Diehl and Ted Rush.

Time to Relax

Finally, in the last few weeks before your wedding, take time out for yourselves. Have your hair and nails done, go for a massage and sauna, do some fun shopping, perhaps even get away for a weekend if your pocketbook and schedule allows it. With all of the excitement generated around the wedding plans, it is important that you take the time to reflect on your relationship and marriage, and to enjoy each other's company. You should also take the time to do things individually if you wish. Spend time with your friends, or just to be alone, doing the things you enjoy most. You've probably spent a lot of time and energy planning a wedding, not only for yourselves, but also for the people with whom you've chosen to share it. You deserve now to spend a little of that time and energy just on yourselves and each other!

❧ 20 ❧

The Big Day!

THERE MAY HAVE BEEN TIMES WHEN YOU didn't think you would get this far, but you've made it! It's now the day before your wedding. You may be a little (or a lot) nervous. You may be going over and over lists to make sure that you haven't forgotten anything. You may even be obsessing over the flowers, the music, the food . . . but do try to relax!

In order to insure that you do relax and enjoy yourselves the day before your wedding, think about planning an activity in advance. Arrange to spend time alone together, if that is your preference, or time with close friends. If you do not already have a rehearsal dinner scheduled, perhaps you would like to get together one last time with your wedding party. If you are close to your families, maybe you'd like to spend time with them, either together or individually. Whatever you choose to do, be sure it is something *you* want to do—something that is relaxing and pleasurable.

If you are living together, one or both of you might consider returning "home" (to your parents' houses) the night before your wedding. Make sure that your clothes are prepared and ready to slip on. The bride should also assemble her makeup and hair necessities so that she doesn't have to scramble to find things in the morning.

She may also want to put together a small bag of cosmetics and other essentials to take along for the day. Both of you should also gather the things you will need on your wedding day, such as fees and tips in envelopes that are clearly marked for the appropriate people; your marriage license/certificate; your rings; clothes to change into if necessary; and everything you will need for your honeymoon, if you plan to leave directly from the reception.

Although it may be difficult, try to get a good night's sleep. If you are feeling anxious or jittery, take a hot bath and try some relaxation techniques: lie in bed, close your eyes, and breathe deeply and steadily. Inhale through your nose to the count of four, and exhale to the count of eight. Try to empty your mind of all thoughts—just concentrate totally on your breathing. You might also try falling asleep to some mellow music or relaxation tapes of ocean or forest sounds. The subtle monotony of these types of tapes should help to lull you to sleep.

Your Wedding Day

On the day of your wedding, wake up slowly and take a relaxing bath or shower. Although your stomach may protest, do try to eat a light meal to carry you through the day and prevent your feeling dizzy. Remember that your reception may be so active that you might not have a chance to eat anything substantial.

Allow yourselves at least an hour to get dressed. The bride may want to do her hair—or have the hairdresser come to the house—first thing in the morning. Depending on whether you will be taking pictures prior to the ceremony, you will need to pace yourselves accordingly. You might want to ask your honor attendants to be in charge of making sure that all of the attendants are ready on time.

The Big Day!

You will probably arrive at the ceremony site approximately forty-five to sixty minutes prior to the start of the ceremony. During this time you will take pictures, greet the ceremony official, and sign the marriage certificate. In the case of a Conservative or Orthodox Jewish ceremony, you will probably need to arrive even earlier in order to participate in certain prenuptial rituals. The nature of your ceremony will determine the time you should arrive, and your official will be able to help you with this.

The music will start approximately thirty minutes before the ceremony is set to begin. Your guests will mingle and find seats; the ushers may escort women or just be on hand to help anyone if it is necessary. Don't forget to give your rings to the appropriate honor attendants. Give the fee envelope to the groom's honor attendant so that he can present it to the official after the ceremony. Your honor attendants can sign your marriage certificate as witnesses.

If your parents will not be walking down the aisle with you, the groom's parents should be escorted to their seats five minutes before the ceremony. Just before the processional, the bride's mother should be escorted to her seat and the ushers will roll out the aisle runner if necessary.

It is common to feel overwhelmed on your wedding day—you might almost feel removed from the experience, as if you are there in body but your mind is a million miles away. Some people don't even remember much of what happened on their special day. Take a few minutes before the ceremony begins to calm your nerves and gather your thoughts. As you walk down the aisle and your ceremony begins, try to focus on exactly what you are doing: your movements, the words being spoken, the people who are sharing this moment with you, the love and joy surrounding you. This is *your* day— relax and enjoy it!

I hope this book has helped you plan your wedding efficiently, and that the process has been smooth. You've probably used the tools of communication and compromise along the way, and now you'll be adept at using them in your marriage too. I wish you a joyous wedding, and hope that the spirit of your special day continues your whole life through.